Sport Climbing with
Robyn Erbesfield

Sport Climbing
with
Robyn Erbesfield

Robyn Erbesfield and Steve Boga

Photographs by Philippe POULET

STACKPOLE
BOOKS

Published by
STACKPOLE BOOKS
5067 Ritter Road
Mechanicsburg, PA 17055

Printed in the United States of America

10 9 8 7 6 5 4 3 2 1

First edition

Cover design by Caroline Stover
Illustrations by Thomas Aubrey

Library of Congress Cataloging-in-Publication Data

Erbesfield, Robyn.
    Sport climbing with Robyn Erbesfield / Robyn Erbesfield and Steve Boga. — 1st ed.
      p. cm.
    ISBN 0-8117-2930-3 (alk. paper)
    1. Rock climbing. 2. Erbesfield, Robyn. I. Boga, Steve, 1947- . II. Title.
    GV200.2.E73 1996
    796.5'223—dc20   96-41660
                                               CIP

Acknowledgments

I can't begin to list the countless people who have assisted me along the way, but I'd like to say one big thank-you to my family and friends. They've helped me to become the athlete that I am today, and the person that I will always be.

Contents

An Important Note to Readers

This book contains much useful information about the sport of rock climbing. Before engaging in this potentially hazardous sport, however, you must do more than read a book.

The sport requires skill, concentration, physical strength and endurance, proper equipment, knowledge of fundamental principles and techniques, and unwavering commitment to your own safety and that of your companions.

The publisher and authors obviously cannot be responsible for your safety. Because rock climbing entails the risk of serious and even fatal injury, we emphasize that you should not begin climbing except under expert supervision. No book can substitute for proper training and experience under the guidance and supervision of a qualified teacher.

Introduction

*Behold the turtle. He makes progress only when
he sticks his neck out.*

—James B. Conant

Growing up in Atlanta, Georgia, I was a dedicated tomboy, an active
kid who liked to play sports—mostly basketball, gymnastics, and soccer—but also liked to hang out with the boys playing kick the can.

When I was a junior in high school, I liked a senior guy named
Philip Fisher, who was a climber. We both had an assignment to put
together a window display of something that appealed to us. I dis-
played baseball hats; he showcased climbing equipment—ropes, nuts,
and Friends.

I noticed that at lunchtime he liked to climb the cracks in the brick
wall around the school. I thought that was pretty cool, so I watched
from a distance for a while, then tried it myself. I enjoyed it, so I asked
Philip to take me climbing at the local crag.

Thus, my climbing career began with my getting my butt pushed
up a 5.8. I couldn't do the first move because the hold was too far
away. But after some friends helped me over that hump, I was able to
climb the route by pulling up on a series of jugs. I could hear guys saying, "Hey, she's good," but I really didn't know what I was doing.

It wasn't that I had heaps of natural talent, but rather that I was a
tomboy and they weren't used to seeing that. I was always in jeans
and a T-shirt, and somehow it was no big deal for me to climb up 5.8
buckets.

Enraptured by this new sport, I was soon bringing at least as much
intensity to it as Philip was. We regularly went climbing on weekends
and bouldering twice during the week. When we weren't visiting

crags, we would go down to the local bar and traverse back and forth along its stone wall. We attached wooden squares to the rafters in Philip's garage and climbed on those. We had pull-up contests and pegboard contests. As a team, we progressed rapidly.

I've always been an intense person, and that quality was reflected in the way I took to climbing. Right from the beginning, I wanted to climb a lot. After a few months, I had gone from not even knowing what climbing was to being pretty good. With that came the realization that if I worked hard I could be very good.

I graduated from high school, wearing my gown and climbing shoes, which Philip had done a year earlier, and his best friend Scott Sanders had done the year before that. Then, a little over a year after taking up climbing and taking up with Philip, he and I moved to Boulder, Colorado, to get away from home and be in the mountains. We spent the first month climbing in famed Eldorado Canyon, fueling our passion for the sport. Then financial reality set in and we had to get jobs. I worked as a receptionist in a real estate office and Philip worked in an auto parts store. It wasn't long before youth and homesickness drove us back to Atlanta.

Between the ages of twenty and twenty-four, I split my time between education and climbing. While I was still in school, I started my own business, a commercial cleaning company called Dust Busters, and for the next few years I spent 50 percent of my time running the business and the other 50 percent trying to be the best climber I could be.

Climbing mostly in Alabama, Tennessee, Georgia, and North Carolina, I continued to refine my skills. From 1986 through 1988, I won the annual Southeastern Bouldering Championships. The competition wasn't all that prestigious, mostly because Lynn Hill and Bobbi Bensman didn't participate. But it gave me some confidence and a taste of competition. In fact, except for a 1988 Masters event at Snowbird, Utah, it was my only competition until I went to Europe for the first World Cup circuit. The Snowbird event was what my family calls a sad joke. My dad was there to videotape me, and he likes to say that before he could get the camera up, I had already fallen.

Still, 1989 was a turning point for me. In April, I was invited to be on the U.S. Climbing Team in sport climbing's first World Cup event, in Leeds, England. But the invitation was for the B team, second string behind Lynn Hill and Bobbi Bensman. Although it was disappointing, the seeding was no doubt legitimate—Lynn and Bobbi were strong climbers, Lynn had already competed in Europe, and both were certainly better known than Robyn Erbesfield.

But then, just before I was to leave for England, Todd Skinner called and asked if I'd be interested in competing for the Alaska Climbing Team—on the A level. I immediately said yes, knowing and caring nothing about the tangled web of politics. I merely saw it as a chance to skip the qualifying rounds and go directly to the quarterfinals. Although it was certainly against the rules to have both an Alaskan team and a U.S. team, the sport was so new that they got away with it—the one and only time.

Given a loophole, I ran with it—or rather, climbed with it— winning that first World Cup event. I remember standing on the podium afterward, thinking, "This is not possible . . . This is not possible." I'd hoped to finish tenth or fifteenth and then reevaluate my goals and aspirations in the sport. But first place removed all doubts. Influenced by the $8,000 in my pocket (from both prize money and sponsor bonuses), I suddenly had a new outlook. Just like that, I was a professional climber.

The other major international competition besides the World Cup is called the Masters. Organizers invite the world's top ten women and top fifteen men for an annual sport climbing competition. In 1989 there was a Masters in Paris, three weeks after the World Cup. Anonymous as I was, I hadn't been invited. But after my victory at Leeds, event officials felt compelled to invite me. A week before the event, they tracked me down in the south of France and did just that.

And I won that one too. I was, as they say, on a roll. Things soon calmed down—I finished third in the next World Cup event, first again in Bulgaria, and either third or fourth in the remaining six events. It was good enough, however, for me to conclude that I had potential.

I entered a new, exciting phase of my life, filled with travel and competitions and new friends. I began to spend more and more time in Europe, where most of the World Cup events are held.

In 1990 I went to Colorado to train with Rob Candelaria, the owner of the Colorado Athletic Training School in Boulder and one of the few people in the country with the talent and experience to teach rock climbing. We worked specifically on improving my ability to compete. It was great preparation for the 1990 World Cup season.

In 1990 I returned to Europe for the circuit. Lynn Hill and I rented

Climbing in competition.

Robyn Erbesfield, World Cup champion in 1995.

a house together in La Tour-d'A'gues, France. She tied for first place with Isabelle Patissier, and I was third.

In 1991 I was again third overall. That year I met Didier Raboutou, a world-class climber, and two years later we were married. We now live in France, returning to the United States about five times a year to compete, teach, and see family. France—and Didier—have been good for my climbing. I have found my soulmate and a place I like to live, which have added stability to my life and made me a stronger climber. So much so that in 1992 I began another, longer roll, winning the first of four straight World Cup titles.

Climbing remains an all-consuming passion for me. For years, everything I've done from the time I get up in the morning—stretching, going for a run, scheduling my entire day—has been built around being a better climber. It's been a wonderful—albeit somewhat restricted—life and I have no regrets. Although my climbing days are not over, I'm interested in turning the page from competition to explore other areas of the sport, such as writing this book, teaching, coaching, course setting, and making films. When I'm not climbing,

I like to hike, especially where I live. Our town is famous for outdoor activities like hiking, mountain biking, canoeing, and kayaking—even caving. Most of my rest days are spent working in my office, outside in the garden or enjoying the outdoor activities around my home.

My progression as a climber was, in many ways, typical. At first I was a weekend warrior, whether it was traditional climbing, bouldering, or traversing the stone wall at the local bar. I started at 5.8, and as I got better, I did some first ascents. By age twenty-one I was doing 5.12a, and when I went to Europe for the first time in 1989 I did my first 5.12d on-sight. In 1990 I redpointed my first 5.13a, and I've since done two 5.14a's. On-sight, I've done one 13c and several 13b's.

As for Philip, he is married, lives in North Carolina, and is still an addicted climber.

After all, we climbers do it for life.

– 1 –

History

Well done is better than well said.

—BEN FRANKLIN

Sport climbing is the one climbing subsport that is truly new, not just the same activity made harder. Its roots can be traced to speed-climbing competition in the late seventies in Russia and Eastern Europe. But speed climbing generated little interest on the other side of the Iron Curtain.

Then in 1985 the Italians held the first sport-climbing event in Bardonecchia. Beset with rain delays and environmental damage, the competition soon moved inside. Sport climbing began to attract thousands of paying spectators, prompting promoters to conclude that there was a future in such events.

They were right, largely because sport climbing is exciting to watch and fun to do. Its growth in the last decade has been exponential. America's first commercial indoor climbing gym, the Vertical Club, opened in Seattle in 1987. The following year, the first major climbing competition was held on American soil at Snowbird, Utah. And in 1989 the World Cup circuit was started, with most of its venues in Europe.

In a 1990 summary of the state of the sport for *Summit* magazine, Lynn Hill correctly observed that "in just the past decade, sport climbing has sprouted into an entirely new branch of rocksport. Dedicated to pure athletic performance, it's the gymnastic pursuit of freeclimbing difficulty on safely protected routes, whether it's putting up a superb new line, repeating a testpiece, winning a competition, or simply climbing for a great workout." Lynn predicted that "the next break-through in sport climbing will see a whole new generation of young climber-athletes competing for gold at the 1996 Olympics." I believe that Lynn's definition of sport climbing is correct; however, I still believe that it will remain a mature sport and the hardest climbs and dominating victories will belong to the climbers with the most experience and hard training.

Although Lynn's Olympic prediction was a tad premature, competition climbing has in fact been recognized by the International Olympic Committee as a "discipline," an interim ranking on the way to official Olympic status. Meanwhile, television coverage continues to grow. The 1994 and 1995 U.S. National Sport Climbing Championships, World Championships, and World Cup events were aired on ESPN. Indoor climbing gyms, nonexistent in the United States ten years ago, have swelled, as of this writing, to 350, with about a thousand more in the works. Some of those gyms are reporting as many as ten thousand new visitors per year. Many people who once lifted weights or took aerobics classes for exercise are turning to sport climbing for recreation and fitness.

One of the key benefits of indoor climbing gyms is their accessibility. An hour after getting off work you can experience climbing, regardless of the hour, season, or weather. You can take a lesson, learn to move freely, get to the top of a wall, lower off, catch someone falling, fall yourself, and have a great time.

– 2 –

Equipment

*The quality of a person's life is in direct
proportion to their commitment to excellence,
regardless of their chosen field of endeavor.*
                                           —VINCE LOMBARDI

Because sport climbers perform their art on prebolted routes, equipment needs are considerably less than those of traditional climbers and dramatically less than those of aid climbers. A good starting kit for sport climbing would include the following:

Daypack or Day-and-a-Half Pack
This should have outer pockets for ready access to water and snacks.

Quickdraws
These are slings with carabiners attached to both ends. I usually carry twelve to fifteen on my rack. One lightweight model carabiner is called Spirit with the gate angled for easy clipping.

Daypack.

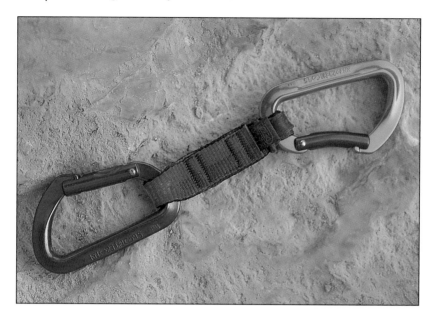

Quickdraws can be used to quickly clip bolts to the leader's rope (*above*). Carabiners clip climbers to belays and ropes to anchors (*bottom left*). The Grigri's self-locking system jams the rope to a stop when the rope is pulled sharply (*bottom right*).

A harness keeps the body upright when rappelling and distributes the shock of a fall.

Belay Device

You'll need a belay device, such as a figure eight, with a locking-gate carabiner. I use a Grigri, a self-locking belay device made by Petzl, which is ideal for sport climbing. If you follow the directions, it's foolproof.

Harness

A lightweight model is fine for sport climbing, because you won't be sitting in it all day doing dozens of pitches. I use Petzl's Crux.

Chalk Bag

The chalk bag should not be too big, but big enough so that you're not fighting to get your hand in.

Colored chalks—standard chalk combined with natural pigments designed to match the rock—are available both loose and in balls. Some climbers claim that colored chalks don't work as well, and the wrong color can be just as unsightly as white. I use the old faithful white block chalk.

Rope

When indoor climbing, sometimes you must bring your own lead rope

A chalk bag.

and sometimes the gym provides it. There are plenty of rope brands made specifically for indoor climbing. Indoors or out, a 10-millimeter or 10.5-millimeter rope is ideal for sport climbing. I suggest Rivory Joanny's Mystic 10.5-millimeter, which is good for indoor, outdoor, top roping, or leading. For climbers whose emphasis is outside and 5.11 and up, consider the Virus 10.2-millimeter. For strictly gym work, I recommend the Super Force 11-millimeter.

Rock Shoes

Ask twelve different climbers which rock shoe is best and you'll probably get a dozen different answers. Because of different climbing styles, preferences, and foot shapes, we all have shoes we swear by and others we disdain.

I recommend two general types. One is a laceless slipper that easily slips on and off, making it practical for gym climbing and bouldering. You will also want a lace-up shoe for competition and outdoor climbing. I use a supple shoe that is made for precise foot placement.

If you're just starting out, your shoe-buying questions will be pretty basic: "Is the shoe durable? Does the rand meet the sole rubber cleanly? Will the shoe do what I want it to? What do I want it to do? Do the colors clash with my outfit?"

First, decide what you want the shoe to do. Most indoor climbers prefer a soft smearing shoe that feels like their own skin. It should be

Look for a shoe that is durable and comfortable.

able to toe into the occasional pocket hold, but mostly it must be a good toe- and heel-hooking shoe.

Many climbs, especially overhangs, demand that you use the heel or toe as a third appendage to grab and pull on holds. Most any shoe will allow you to latch on to a large knob or ledge, but for a slim edge or sloper, you need more sticky rubber surrounding the heel. Look also for a deep heel box—you don't want the shoe popping off during a power hook—and a soft heel counter that is pliable enough to wrap around holds and let you feel the rock.

Not so long ago, climbers suffered in shoes several sizes smaller than their street-shoe size. Today, most quality shoes perform well even if they're only slightly tighter than your street shoes. In any event, sizing varies with each manufacturer, so rely on feeling rather than a number.

Shoes for sport climbing should fit very tightly, usually one and a half to two sizes below your street shoe size. Such a fit will be painful at first, and you'll probably tolerate them only for short stints. After a week or two, the shoes will break in and become more comfortable, although if you find yourself wearing them when belaying or hiking, they are undoubtedly too large. Remember that shoes will stretch after a while, and supertight shoes will stretch more than moderately tight ones.

When you try on shoes at your local mountain shop, try to do it barefoot. If rules prohibit it or you have a major foot fungus, wear only a thin liner sock. Try the shoes on, and wear them around the shop as long as you can. Don't be pressured by pushy salespeople; find a reputable shop where the salespeople are knowledgeable and informative.

Because of the vagaries of sizing, avoid mail-order shoes unless you know the size from previous experience with that company or are prepared to send them back. Once you have your shoes home, wear them around on the carpet to make certain you have made the right choice. If not, simply return them. Reputable shops will exchange the shoes as long as you haven't climbed in them.

It is important to get the right rock shoes, so do your research. Most climbing magazines do an annual shoe report, rating popular brands on such things as friction, edging, and durability. Also, try to stop by your local climbing gym when it is hosting shoe demonstrations; this will allow you to see and test shoes before you buy them and to talk with other climbers about what works best for them. Ultimately, however, you must decide for yourself.

Clothing

Climbing imposes no dress code, so dress for comfort. I usually wear shorts or tights. If it's hot and I'm outside doing knee-locks, I wear loose-fitting pants cut below the knee for extra protection. If I'm in the gym and not doing knee-locks, I usually wear shorts. Verve makes excellent shorts for sport climbing that are durable and fit well beneath the harness.

Above the waist, I wear a tank top or T-shirt when climbing indoors and, depending on the weather, layers outdoors.

– 3 –

Techniques and Tactics

I am only one; but still I am one.
I cannot do everything, but still I can do something;
I will not refuse to do the something I can do.
—HELEN KELLER

Good technique, the key to efficient climbing, will allow you to use less than your maximum strength, especially on powerful moves. By saving this energy, your endurance will also improve.

When learning new skills, take it slow and practice only good technique. If you start to feel sloppy, stop and rest or revert to something easier. Return to the harder climb when you're fresh and full of energy. Quality is more important than quantity when learning new techniques or trying to progress.

The purpose of this chapter is to teach you how to climb well—even when the going gets tough. That may seem obvious, but too many people concentrate on gaining power and endurance and forget about their real goal: climbing well. Instead of focusing on proper body position and precise hand- and footwork, too many climbers simply do whatever it takes to get to the top. If I watch someone reputed to be the strongest in the gym, I often see a guy thugging his way to the top. Maybe he tops out on a 5.12, but his style was hideous. If he would learn to climb well, with grace and precision, he'd be doing 5.13 three months later.

What I mean by climbing well is making good decisions, positioning the body correctly, and developing rhythm. When you analyze good climbing, breaking it down to its basics, you see that it's made up of precise body movements. But to a lot of people who believe that the end justifies the means, climbing is simply muscling their way to the top. If the musclers would concentrate on the basics—precise handwork, precise footwork, and using momentum—they could advance to a new level without any more power or stamina.

No matter how talented you are, you are bound to hit developmental plateaus, periods of stagnation when progress seems nil. When that happens, look for new tools. Talk to other climbers, attend clinics, focus on the areas of stagnation. A common error for intermediates is trying to climb routes too difficult for their ability. The result is forced moves instead of graceful ones. Return to the basics and try to perfect climbing at a moderate level. This doesn't mean you can't work hard routes, because hard routes help you gain power. But it does mean breaking down the route into individual moves and trying to do each correctly.

Foot Techniques

Beginners have to overcome the temptation to pull, rather than push, their way up climbs. Too often they want to grab everything with their hands, dragging the feet up almost as an afterthought.

Yet your leg muscles are some of the strongest in the body, and the more weight you can put on your feet, the less you have to tax your upper-body muscles. Emphasize footwork by changing the placement of your feet before moving your hands; then try moving your foot placements twice before moving your hands. Alternate between two basic rhythms: foot, foot, hand, foot, foot, hand; and foot, hand, foot, hand. Note how moving even one foot to a higher hold enables you to reach higher.

Go out of your way on easy routes to use small or irregular footholds. Try to place your feet on the best part of each hold. With your hands on big holds, seek out tiny, irregular footholds and test how much weight each type of hold—and each part of a hold—will support. As you gain a feel for what your feet can do, try this exercise on different kinds of rock with smaller and smaller handholds. Relax your grip and let your feet support most of your weight.

On top rope, climb a low-angle slab, using your hands only for balance by pushing with your palms. After a while, you will be able to ascend steeper faces with no hands as long as the footholds are big. This will teach you to trust your feet when handholds are few and far between.

Climb quietly and aim for precise foot placements. Try to avoid scraping the wall before placing your foot on the proper hold. Raise your leg, then pause an instant before final placement to orient the foot.

A flagged foot can give you better balance and reach.

This will improve precision and build strength. Follow your foot with your eyes until it is placed precisely on the hold. Once it's placed, try not to move it. As your climbs become harder, keeping your feet steady and being precise will be more critical, as even slight movements or changes in pressure can cause a slip.

As you become more advanced, you will learn to *flag* your feet for better balance and reach. In this technique, one foot, known as the flagged foot, is not placed on a foothold but rather is splayed out to the side or behind you. The flagged foot may touch the rock or hang in the air; it may pass behind or in front of the standing leg. Practice by looking for flag moves on a moderate route.

Work on precise foot placement by using a hold exactly as you first contact it. Even if it's an awkward hold, stay with it. This will force you to concentrate on your feet and make good decisions. Start this exercise on easy routes, so that you can concentrate fully on your feet.

Edging: inside (*top*) and
outside (*middle*).

Edging. With this
technique, you butt
the edge of your
shoe—the tip, the
inside edge by the big
toe, the outside edge,
or even the heel—onto
a rock edge. Imagine
trying to stand on a
miniature ledge with
the edge of your shoe.

Look for the best possible foot position. Changing from an adequate outside edge to a very good inside edge can conserve energy and make the climb easier.

Smearing. Smearing is used on slopes that lack definite edges. You should place your foot on the part of the rock that slopes the least, laying as much sole rubber onto the rock or hold as possible. Now distribute your weight over as much surface area of the shoe as you can.

Smearing uses friction instead
of definite edges to hold the
sole to rock.

Look for bumps, tiny edges, and other rough spots that can improve the security of a smear.

Of course, this technique isn't really new to you. You use smearing in everyday life when you walk up even a slight hill. It's really just a matter of spreading your weight over a large area and making maximum use of the static friction created by the rubber sole against the rock.

Heel and Toe Hooks. A heel hook can be effective on larger holds, where you maneuver one leg almost as a third arm. Heel hooks are especially useful when turning a roof. A similar technique is the toe hook. On overhangs, a toe pull may be useful. In a toe pull, you use

the toe of your shoe as you would use your fingers to pull up on an undercling.

You can also play with a toe and heel hook at the same time. This counterbalance provides a nice rest.

Back Stepping. Back stepping is most useful when you have to reach a hold far away. Place one or both feet on the outside edge of the shoes and slightly behind you, keeping your hip close to the wall, and reach for the hold. If possible, drop your inside knee and lower your hip, bringing your body closer to the

A heel hook (*top*), and a double toe hook (*bottom*).

wall. Dropping your knee further positions your body closer to the wall, placing less stress on your arms.

Knee-Drop. The knee-drop is an exaggerated back step, in which the outside leg is straight and the inside foot is on a high foothold with the knee bent and lowered.

High-Step. The high-step is used to reach footholds that are high up, usually around your

A back step can help you reach a hold far away (*right*). A knee-drop is an exaggerated back step (*bottom left*). The bent knee is important in this technique (*bottom right*).

hips. Because it takes more energy than a regular move, you should use the high-step only when there are no closer footholds, unless the next hand hold is far away.

Hand Techniques

There are two general ways to grab knobs, protrusions, pockets,

edges, or slopes with the fingers: *crimping* and *open-hand* positions. Whether you crimp, use an open-hand technique, or something in between, always remember to conserve energy and never pull harder than you have to. Try to apply only the necessary pressure on each hold.

Crimping is a good way to grab small holds (*left*). A two-finger pocket hold (*bottom left*). A semi-crimp (*bottom right*).

Crimping. Crimping involves grabbing a hold so that the fingers are in a scrunched-up position. Usually it's necessary to crimp the worst holds, like small, dime-size edges and incut flakes. Crimping requires more strength, uses the thumb more, stresses the tendons of the hands more, and puts them at greater risk for injury than open-hand tech-

niques. Experiment with different holds to find the right position for you. Vary your grip so that you tax different muscles.

Open-Hand Techniques. *Semi-Crimping.* If you face a little larger, or positive, hold, open-hand the hold, as it lets more of the skeletal system of the hand bear your weight. Take the hold with an open, relaxed hand, as you would a chin-up bar or the rung of a ladder. In this position, your fingers will be half bent.

Palming. Palming—putting the entire palm, or maybe the last three knuckles, straight in on the rock—is used on bigger holds or sloppers. It relies on the friction between the rock and the skin of the palm or fingers, and is usually used with an inward and downward push that works the triceps (dips are a good training exercise). A palming hold may be quite tenuous, because the slightest movement of the hand can break the friction.

Underclinging. An undercling

Palming (*top*), like smearing, relies on friction between climber and rock. Underclinging (*below*).

Laybacking is useful in climbing cracks and arêtes.

is a hold that is usually horizontal and taken with the hand in an inverted position. Underclings can vary from tiny to huge. They are sometimes difficult to spot, but they can be the key to reaching the next hold, particularly if it is far away. When underclinging, look for the best foot placement; often a high placement is better than a low one. Try varying your hand placements, looking for the best ones. Sometimes crimping with your thumb can make things a lot easier.

Laybacking. Not all hand techniques require a downward pull. At times it is necessary to use side pulls or even upward pulls, depending on body positioning and the move you are attempting. Laybacking is grabbing a vertical edge, often a flake of rock, then pulling with the hands, pushing with the feet, and walking the feet up almost alongside the hands. It is a strenuous but useful technique for arêtes, corners with cracks, and cracks offset in walls. Laybacks, or horizontal holds, are usually crimped, though they may be taken open-handed if large enough. Make good decisions when choosing footholds for opposition.

Leading

Climber Craig Luebben once said that "the full joy of climbing is found only on the sharp end." He was talking about leading, the most exhilarating and risky part of climbing.

Although sport climbing is the safest form of climbing, don't be lulled into a false sense of security. Leader and belayer must still thread the right loops and tie the right knots. And some bolted routes have major runouts, with the distance between two bolts sufficient to cause a groundfall if the leader falls near the upper bolt—especially

When leading a bolted route, it's important to remember the saying "into the wall, out to the climber." The process is simple—clip one carabiner of a quickdraw into the bolt, then clip the rope into the other carabiner. Just make sure that both carabiner gates face away from your direction of travel.

after pulling 8 feet of slack. In such cases, it's safer to clip the bolt near your waist.

Placing protection on bolted routes is straightforward: The leader clips one carabiner of the quickdraw into the bolt, then the rope into the other carabiner. Both carabiner gates should face away from the anticipated direction of travel. For example, if you plan to move past the protection to the left, orient both carabiner gates so that they face to the right. Remember the saying "Into the wall, out to the climber." Clip the rope so that it goes up and out through the carabiner to your harness instead of up and in through the carabiner.

Build confidence in your ability to lead by starting easy and working up slowly. For your first sport-climb lead, choose a route at least one full grade below what you can top-rope with no falls. If it's your first time leading, you might want to have your partner leave the quickdraws in place for you to remove; if you have the stamina and reach to unclip the quickdraws on top rope, you should be able to make the clips on lead.

Next, try to lead the route with the draws already in place. Finally, lead the route placing the draws yourself.

Combined Techniques

Reach. Several common body positions are used to make reaches. Each involves pushing with your legs and locking off or turning your body so that the non-reaching hand can help you get to the next hold.

Stem. Also known as bridging, this climbing technique involves pushing out to the sides with hands, feet, or both, using opposing pressure against the rock. Stemming is often used in climbing chimneys or dihedrals.

Dyno. A dyno, or dynamic move, is an explosive move in which one or both of the climber's hands or feet may be disengaged from the rock in order to fly up to the next hold.

Cross-through. Although it is not used often, the cross-through is a fun and photogenic way to traverse. With the right leg directly below you and supporting your weight, place the left foot on a high hold while keeping your left hand on a hold that is just above your head. Reach far to the left with your right hand (underneath the left hand),

Stemming.

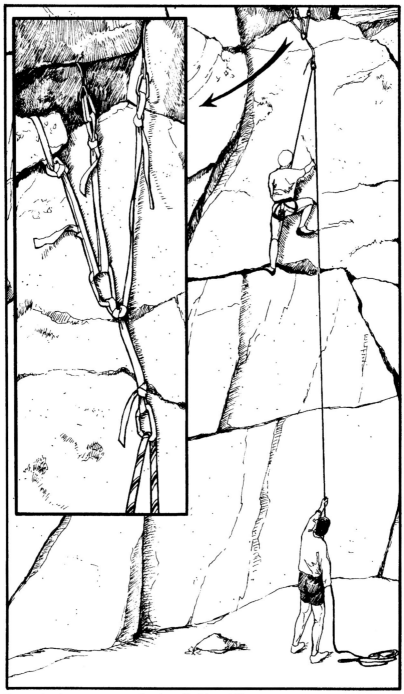

Top roping is a great way to develop climbing skills.

opening your body away from the wall (crossing). Then push off with your right leg and pivot your left foot from an inside to an outside edge. Your weight will transfer from the right side of the body to the left as your hips and shoulders turn to face the wall again (un-crossing). To move to the right, reverse this process.

Top Roping

Top roping, rigging an anchor above the climb or pitch, is a great way to develop physical, gymnastic climbing confidence. There are three basic ways to top-rope a one-pitch climb. One method is to go to the top of the cliff and drop a rope down to another person who can advise the climber from below. Another way is for the leader to lead the climb, fix an anchor at the top, and then bring the next climber up. A third way is to run a rope through an anchor at the top so that the climb can be belayed from below.

Top-roping a one-pitch climb.

For most climbers, leading is the ultimate artistic expression. If you're not ready to get on lead, however, then top roping is a great alternative. If your climbing deteriorates on lead—say from 5.9 to 5.5—you know you will have to work up to it.

One way to improve is to work a route over and over, gaining confidence in your ability to do the moves. Top roping is great for working a route, going bolt to bolt, refining every move. Once you know the moves, you can then try to complete it from bottom to top without falling.

Top roping is also good for doing laps, building stamina. If you want to climb a route over and over, it's not necessary to go up on lead every time. Instead, make the climb, have your partner lower you back down, then repeat the climb. The time you would have spent clipping bolts can now be spent climbing and improving your stamina. On each successive try, if the route is the right difficulty, you will know the moves better but be more fatigued.

Redpointing

Redpointing, climbing a route from bottom to top after rehearsal, is effective for working power. You can usually redpoint much harder routes than you can climb on-sight (see page 23). Rehearsal allows you to find the best position to clip from and correct errors in sequence, technique, hold choice, and pacing. By eliminating those errors, you can approach your maximum potential. That is the allure of the hard redpoint.

I recommend that you work out each section of a redpoint from bolt to bolt. Think of it as working small boulder problems with a rope. (I call it "doing boulder problems in the sky.") Refine each move, then deposit it in your memory bank. Figure out where you're going to put your hands and feet on the third move, whether you outside edge or inside edge on the fifth move, and so on. When you finally solve all those problems and link them together, you will be able to redpoint the route.

If a route is near your limit, you'll get progressively more tired as you ascend. Since fatigue shreds good technique, you will need to practice the higher moves more than the lower ones so that you will have equal competence on both.

Flashing

The term flashing is often misused in the United States. To flash a route is to watch someone else do that route, then do it yourself for the first time. If you flash a 5.14a, I'm impressed; if you on-sight a 5.14a, I'm even more impressed.

Flashing can be a stepping stone to better performance. You watch someone do certain moves, remember what they've done, then do it yourself. In one sense, it's not too different from what you face in competition—you have to remember moves and imitate them.

One possible pitfall: I may watch a tall person do a sequence of moves, then find out once I'm up there that it doesn't work for me.

On-sighting

Climbing a route with no prior knowledge, besides what you can absorb during a brief observation period, is a climber's ultimate challenge. It's what you face in most competitions, so you definitely want to practice on as many on-sights as possible.

Give yourself about six minutes to observe, trying to gain and store as much information as possible from the ground. Then walk away from the climb and think about it; run it through your mind and be ready to start the climb with as much information as possible. Practicing the six-minute observation period will develop your imagination and ability to read routes, and make you a better on-sight competitor.

Belaying

To belay is to tend the climbing rope, ready to immediately put enough friction on it to hold the climber in case of a fall. Friction is generated by the rope passing through a belay device. Belaying is the primary safeguard in climbing, and its practice is universal.

Belaying in sport climbing is magnified in importance by the large number of falls that sport climbers regularly take. The average sport

A good belayer's duties begin even before the leader leaves the ground. The capable belayer will stack the rope with the lead end on top, making sure that no knots or kinks interfere with a smooth belay. The belayer should also make sure that the leader has enough gear clipped to her harness. And she should check the leader's knot and harness before she starts climbing. Good sport climbers regularly check each other's knots and belay setups. You are, after all, a team.

Prepare for a smooth belay by stacking the rope free of knots or kinks.

If the route features difficult moves before the first bolt, a good belayer will spot the leader until she gets the first bolt clipped. That may give the leader the confidence she needs to succeed, and it gets the belayer into the habit of watching the climber.

As the climber proceeds, the belayer should be stationed as directly under the first bolt as possible to avoid a groundfall or a pendulum. Maintain your focus by continually running through your mental checklist: Verify that the belay biner is locked. Watch the leader to make sure she clips bolts correctly, that she keeps the rope in front of her legs, that she is in no apparent danger. Try to stay one step ahead of the leader, anticipating her clips and falls.

Since clipping bolts on sport routes can be strenuous, the belayer must make available enough rope to clip quickly but not so much that the climber hits the deck if she falls. In general, the belayer should keep about one full reach of rope loose in the system (assuming the climber is high enough to avoid a groundfall). This allows the leader to pull up one full reach without having to give the belayer any warning. When the leader clips a bolt higher than her harness, the belayer should temporarily take in the slack to keep the rope out of her way and to avoid an unnecessarily long fall.

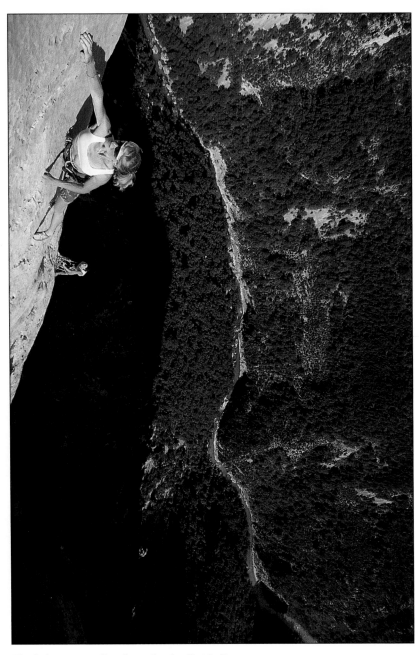

The belayer stays directly under the first bolt.

Belay Devices. Figure-eight rings were designed for rappelling, not belaying. Nevertheless, the figure eight is an often-used belay device that is effective, provided the belayer knows how to use it and never takes her brake hand off the rope.

The recent invention of a self-locking belay device has made belaying even easier. It contains an integral security system that locks on to the climber's rope when the rope is pulled sharply. It's similar to an automobile seat belt: When movement is slow, the rope runs freely through the device; when shock load is reached, the Grigri locks, jamming the rope to a stop. In contrast, a falling climber who is belayed with a figure eight faces the risk that his belayer will react slowly to a fall, causing rope burn and release of rope. Of course, this should never happen if the belayer pays close attention to her brake hand.

Like most things in life, the Grigri is foolproof only if you use it correctly. Keep in mind the following:

- When the Grigri is in use, the belayer should always hold on to the back rope, as with any belay device.
- Feed the rope through the Grigri with two hands. Using small movements, push the rope through the back end and pull it out the front end. The metal face is embossed with a diagram showing which end of the rope goes to the climber and which end goes to the belayer. Be gentle or the device will lock. Practice it until you are smooth.
- When the lead climber wants to rest, the belayer lightly grips the back rope with one hand and the Grigri takes the weight. Because the belayer doesn't have to hold the weight or tie off, as with other belay devices, he gets a rest too.
- The Grigri does not provide a dynamic belay. It stops a fall quickly and surely, with no slippage. For this reason, Petzl says, "We do not recommend the use of the Grigri in any situation where there is doubt about the strength of the anchor points. On well-protected routes and in gyms, where the anchors comply with the UIAA standard, the Grigri may be used with confidence."
- The Grigri is not effective on ropes smaller than 10 millimeters. It was designed for dynamic ropes with diameters of 10 to 11 millimeters.
- In case of a fall, belayers must resist the temptation to clamp both hands on the lead rope going to the climber. This could

delay the Grigri locking action. (Even with a figure eight or a Sticht plate, this is a bad technique that can result in burned hands, a released rope, and a falling climber.) Instead, hold the back rope with one hand, using moderate force.

- In case of a fall, avoid grabbing both ropes together in one hand, a common procedure with other belay devices. The pressure of the hand against the Grigri may, in the words of Petzl, "impede its proper function and prevent it from stopping the fall."

Falling

Yes, falling is a skill, one you need to learn and practice. Fear of falling is natural. Toss a baby up in the air, and before you can catch her, her face is contorted in fear. We have to learn to challenge that fear, to control it. In sport climbing, it's not so much the fall we fear, but the uncertainty. This is why the first fall on a climb is usually the scariest.

In traditional climbing, the adage has long been "The leader must not fall." Because sport climbers fall often, particularly when pushing their level, they must practice and perfect their technique, just as they do with belaying and rappelling. Sport climbers who refuse to fall will never take the chances necessary to progress.

The best way to gain trust in the system is to fall intentionally. Find an overhanging climb with bomber protection, and add a qualified belayer and quality rope. Make sure your knots are properly tied, your carabiners are properly clipped.

Climb up a couple of bolts, tell your belayer, "Falling. Take me," and take a fall. When you feel comfortable with that, make one move past that bolt and say, "Falling." Then two moves, three moves, four moves, and so on. Work up incrementally until you feel comfortable with significant falls.

Boulderers also have to learn incrementally how to fall. When you're secured by a top rope, you can fall with little consequence, but when you're bouldering, you must be able to jump off the problem or know how to fall correctly. Do a single move and take a fall. Do another, and before you know it you're 5 feet up, high enough that a bad landing could do damage. If you make the next move, you will be 7 feet off the ground, which can be intimidating. By practicing, you will know you can fall under control, which will give you the confidence to go on.

Sport climbers must know how to fall properly.

Though no substitute for learning proper falling technique, gymnastic mats make great crash pads. Or make your own by sewing carpet around a thick piece of foam.

Learn to fall so that your body is balanced and upright. The biggest mistake people make is landing with rigid legs. It's better to absorb the impact by going into a squat. As your feet touch the ground, sag into the landing rather than trying to resist the force.

Even experienced climbers can feel fluttery about falling. At the start of a new season, if I haven't been on a rope in a while, I have a little fear that I have to exorcise. During some of the easier climbs, I begin to reflect on inconsequential falls I've taken and remind myself that any fall I might take on this climb will be just as inconsequential. Once I have finished my warm-up, I can put aside falling and concentrate on climbing.

Unplanned falls can be broken into three phases: the moments leading up to separation from the rock; air travel; and possible contact with something hard.

Falls seldom happen without warning. As you hesitate, trying to decide between two moves, you will sense the last few seconds on the pump clock, the energy draining away. During that hiatus, picture the likely direction and force of the fall and consider possible safety measures. When you have a spare moment, alert the belayer and sort out the rope so that it doesn't entangle your legs. If you make it a habit to climb with the rope running in front of your legs, you won't have to fiddle with it while flying through the air. Air time could be better spent analyzing possible impact scenarios with the rock.

Cushion the blow of body against wall and protect your head by interposing your hands and feet. Watch how cats fall for tips. They absorb the impact of landing by spreading it over as many appendages as possible. Most important, stay relaxed and alert.

Mental Techniques

First, clarify your goals. I urge you to focus, first, last, and always, on climbing well. With good climbing, you'll progress. When I compete, I'm trying to climb my very best that particular day, not trying to beat the other climbers. That simplified approach greatly reduces the prevailing stress. I'm just trying to apply the things I've learned in the past, and if I do that, I go home happy.

Consider this athletic equation:

$$Performance = Potential - Interference$$

Performance is how well you actually do—your results. Potential is a measurement of the best performance you are capable of at any given moment. Interference is the mental static produced by the conscious mind.

As pressure mounts, so do self-doubts and anxiety, two other prime causes of mental static. Again, the conscious mind rushes in, usually to provide a litany of advice, much of it negative: "Lock off . . . drop the knee . . . twist . . . no, the other way."

With all that advice raining down on you, it's easy to forget to relax the muscles not on the front lines. And the unwanted contraction of only a few extra muscle fibers in the arms is enough to waste you before your time.

It's clear that a reduction of mental interference will improve performance, even with no change in potential (read: practice). In other words, get your head screwed on right and you can become a better climber.

But the overactive conscious mind does not react well to being told to butt out. (It's rather like ordering yourself to sleep.) Instead, you may have to rely on deceit. Some advise distracting the conscious mind by focusing on something only marginally related to the task at hand. By giving it something else to chew on, the subconscious is left unfettered.

Two good ways to distract that pesky conscious mind are to associate positively and to visualize. Suppose you are facing a challenging dyno, a move with which you've had both good and bad moments. For best results, embrace the successes and discard the failures. Replay an imaginary tape that you might call "My Greatest Hits." Immerse yourself in positive recollections. If you find yourself thinking negatively—"I can't do this dyno"—immediately switch to positive thinking: "I've done this dyno and I can do it again."

Visualization is a type of mental rehearsal in which you conjure up detailed visions of the activity before you do it. The first step is to relax. This should be done alone in a quiet place. Use a method that works for you. You might close your eyes and take a few deep breaths; or recite your favorite mantra. Try focusing on each part of your body and ridding it of tension.

Once you are relaxed, you can begin to focus on the upcoming climb. Immerse yourself in the climb. See it as one fluid whole, then break it down into its parts, the individual moves. Feel the hold each time as it contacts your fingers; note its texture, temperature, shape. Smell the chalk, the rock, the success. See yourself climbing well, fluid and in control, all the way to the belay anchors. Try this three times a week for a month before the real event. If you are redpointing, you may want to visualize the route during the week and redpoint it on the weekend, for example.

Visualization takes dedicated practice. The upside is that you can practice it anywhere—in a bed or bathtub, at a bus stop—and the rewards can be staggering. Research suggests that muscles respond to visualization of an act almost as if you were doing the act. Thus, the more intensely you visualize the perfect move, the more entrenched it will be in your muscle memory. This kind of memory operates almost entirely on the subconscious level, which helps explain how you can do well but can't tell others how you do it.

When fatigue threatens to shock load one part of your system, you need to find ways to disperse it. The following are some suggestions.

- Weight your arms to give your feet and legs a break.
- Alternate fingers in finger pockets.
- Weight your thumb on edges to relieve your fingers.
- Grip buckets with the outer edge of your palm to relieve your fingers.
- Stem to recover arm strength.
- Dyno easier moves down low to preserve your static locking power for a lock-off crux higher up.
- Take advantage of rest spots.
- Try to choose the easiest option for each move, even the easy ones. Follow the line of least resistance.
- Keep a good rhythm throughout the climb, concentrating on using momentum to travel from one move to another.
- Maintain good breathing, which feeds more oxygen to the brain and improves concentration and recovery.

Bouldering

Bouldering is ropeless, solo climbing usually done within jumping distance of the ground. You don't have to untangle a rope, manage hardware, or worry about your belayer's attention span. The challenge is simply to reach the top of a small rock (or the final designated hold when bouldering on a wall), and all you need is a pair of rock shoes, a chalk bag, and nonrestrictive clothing. It is climbing at its basic best.

Bouldering allows you to practice techniques and improve your climbing. Choose an easy boulder problem for learning new techniques. Experiment with the position of your hands, feet, and torso to determine what works best for you. Ask experienced climbers to watch you and evaluate your technique; or watch them and evaluate theirs. As you eliminate flaws and become more consistent, progress to harder boulder problems. Create routes that emphasize your weaknesses more than your strengths. If you are having trouble holding pinches, make up a problem with lots of pinches. Do the same, as needed, with underclings, slopers, or whatever.

Although it can be beneficial to go bouldering by yourself, it's usually more productive to go with other people, especially when you're starting out. You can get valuable input from other climbers, and besides, you may need a spotter. Most people find it easier to push their limits when others are around.

Bouldering success can provide the confidence you need to succeed in competition climbing. It's just so easy to walk up to a boulder problem and work at it for hours. By steadily increasing the difficulty of your boulder problems, you will find that your ability and confidence grow.

If you can do all the boulder problems in your area, it will give you a huge psychological boost when you're on a wall facing a challenging move. You may realize that the move before you is easier than some of the boulder problems you've done. Because of your success doing boulder problems, because of the confidence you've developed, you've made a critical psychological leap. And you're a better climber for it.

Indoor Walls

Artificial climbing walls are now available in many gyms and outdoors stores. There's probably one near you, but if you don't have access to an indoor climbing gym, you can build an artificial wall, use

Bouldering.

someone else's, or work out on a real brick or stone wall. Remember, I used to practice on a local bar's stone wall. It wasn't built for climbing, but it worked for me. I improved strength and technique traversing back and forth on it.

At our home in France, Didier and I have a climbing wall mounted on a conveyor belt that keeps the holds moving and allows you to climb only a foot or two off the ground. We also have our own climbing gym, located at the rear of our property in a building open to the public. It features bouldering and some roped climbing, the latter of which is especially nice for children and beginners. Here we offer clinics to climbers of all levels.

Besides practicing the techniques and tactics we've outlined in this chapter, avail yourself of good instruction; read books, watch others climb, think about what you've seen, break down the movements, ask questions. By making it your goal to climb well, not just to reach the top or to win, you remove a lot of pressure and have more fun.

That is, after all, why you're climbing.

— 4 —

Training

*The difficult things in this world
are solved through motivation.*

—WALT STACK

I'm reluctant to prescribe my training regimen for others because it's so abnormal—grueling, some would say. It works for me, but it may not work for you. After all, my training is geared toward making me the best competitive sport climber in the world. Perhaps you have more modest goals. In any case, avoid diving into a training program that is extremely long or intense. Start at the low end of the spectrum and stay with it. Progressively raise both intensity and duration as you improve.

I divide training into the following categories:

Power—targeted by short sprints of four to ten moves, high intensity.

Short resistance—ten to twenty moves, maybe two boulder problems linked, high intensity.

Long resistance—twenty to thirty-five moves, medium-high intensity.

Stamina—thirty-five to fifty moves, medium-high intensity.

Volume—fifty to eighty moves, medium intensity.

As the number of moves increases, the intensity of the climbing decreases. Power moves are extremely difficult, so you link only a few. On the other hand, a volume workout might be the equivalent of doing a dozen routes. You can't do a dozen 5.14s in a day, so you lower the degree of difficulty to a comfortable level below your limits, and do mileage.

Because climbing demands versatility, it's important to regularly work all five categories. Some coaches recommend working, say, power for four weeks and then moving on to stamina for four weeks.

35

But I believe that if you spend too much time working just one category, you lose too much in the other areas. So if you want to be a well-rounded climber, you should work these five areas to varying degrees every week.

For example, I might work power and long resistance on the first training day, stamina and volume on the next. Each day has a theme, and I concentrate on that theme several hours in a single day and more than once a week.

With this method, you never get too far away from any one facet. In fact, it's not uncommon to work more than one on a single route. For example, you might work a route that has an obvious crux about 10 feet off the ground, which is followed by a rather long and very intense section (long resistance), and finishes with big holds far away making the final push a simple pump.

The next step is to convert these principles into a training schedule that works for you. Into the mix go your goals (world champion, weekend warrior), availability (demands of work, family), nearby resources (crags, climbing gyms), present fitness level (lean and mean, couch potato convert).

For the record, here's what my typical training week might look like when no competition is imminent.

I run flat terrain every other day, or two days on and one day off. My pace is slow and steady for twenty to fifty minutes. Twenty minutes is a warm-up, fifty minutes more of a workout. Running is great for the cardiovascular system, but I mostly use it for recovery and warm-up. I find it really flushes things out.

After the warm-up, I stretch from head to toe. This is critical for increasing flexibility and avoiding injury. (Some exercises are detailed below.)

Next, if it's a bouldering (power) day, I usually do specific finger work on a training board. I also might do sets of pull-ups, both half and full, push-ups, and dips.

Then I move to easy bouldering problems—controlled climbing—before trying anything that could be traumatic to the body. As my movement becomes more fluid, I mix in harder problems. Incidentally, I define a hard bouldering problem as one I can't do on the first try; I have to work it, break down the movements, learn the precise placements necessary to hit holds at the right time and right place.

Also on bouldering days, I mix in what I call a power-endurance (otherwise known as short resistance) workout. It's several boulder problems linked together, or a circuit of ten to fifteen moves. It's very hard from first to last, no shaking out, no resting. I usually make up several circuits and try to link them, resting between tries. Or I link hard routes I already have in place.

As always, I finish with a cool-down that includes stretching and sometimes running for recuperation.

The next day, I work stamina by doing routes with thirty to forty moves. I usually do this for one to three hours, varying the routes. Even my stamina routes are hard. I like to build longer routes that require me to really push myself if I'm going to link them. After that, I work volume, doing several longer, easier routes. I finish with stretching and sometimes running.

After an active rest day (easy running and stretching), I repeat that two-day pattern. And I pretty much do that all the time. It comes to about twenty-five to thirty hours a week and is, for me, time well spent. But, of course, you can have both success and fun climbing with a lesser investment of time. Nevertheless, the basic elements I outlined in my training week should be included in your workout schedule, although perhaps with less intensity.

Let's look at the elements of training in detail.

I award each workout day with one to four stars, four being maximum intensity. If day one is four stars, then day two is three stars. As I approach competition, I'm on one- and two-star days.

A four-star day might look like this:
- 1 hour of warm-up—running and aerobics—and stretching.
- 1 $^1/_2$ to 3 hours of bouldering.
- 2 hours of short or long endurance.
- Cool-down.

Warm-up

Although given short shrift by some athletes who are impatient to dive right into the main feature, a warm-up prepares you for exercise by gradually increasing your heart rate and blood flow, raising the temperature of muscles and connective tissue, and improving muscle function, all of which help reduce the chance of injuries, such as muscle pulls and tendinitis. Without a warm-up, on the other hand, there is less blood flow and muscle elasticity, increasing the chance of injury. In this state, your muscles are "surprised" by sudden movement.

A balanced warm-up is especially important for climbers because the sport is so diversified. Runners know they have to stretch their legs, but what do climbers emphasize? We use both upper and lower body. When I go to a competition, I don't know whether I will confront a big overhang, a roof, a slab, something really short, really long, hard at the start, hard at the end. Accordingly, we must prepare mind and body for everything.

Some people like to begin by stretching, but cold stretching can damage muscles and tendons. Instead, you should start with a more full-body warm-up, such as easy jogging, stationary cycling, or aerobics for five to ten minutes. A light sweat usually indicates that you've warmed up sufficiently.

Stretching

After running or cycling to warm general areas, it's time to stretch the specific areas that climbing stresses. Test and extend your range of motion with slow, gentle, yogalike stretches. Slow, steady stretching increases muscle length very gradually, avoiding the damaging stretch reflex that accompanies sudden movements.

Here's a stretching routine I like to introduce to the students in my climbing seminars:

Start in the standing position, but don't let that keep you from relaxing. Take a few slow, deep breaths. As you inhale, your stomach should swell with air; as you exhale, your stomach should flatten out. I'm a big believer in good breathing habits, especially when climbing. For some reason, when we face a tense or difficult moment, we tend to hold our breath. The quicker you can catch your mistake and return to good breathing, the better. Try to maintain good breathing throughout the following exercises.

Let's start with neck rolls. Slowly, gently, go left to right, forward and backward. Don't forget to breathe. Then move your neck in circles, slowly, gently, relax the parts of the body not being used. Now change directions.

Next, shoulder rolls. Hunch your shoulders, bringing them up toward your ears, then drop them. Relax. Repeat several times.

Stretch your arms out to the sides and rotate them in small circles, then bigger circles, and then even bigger circles. Now change directions.

With your arms straight out in front of you, work your fingers, opening and closing them as though you were shaking off water. Put your arms up, then down to your sides, all the while opening and closing the hands. Don't forget to breathe. Now shake the tension out of your arms.

Neck rolls (*top*) and shoulder rolls (*bottom*).

Clockwise from top left: arm circles, finger work, finger stretch, wrist curl, thumb stretch, shoulder stretch.

Grab your right elbow with your left hand, and bring the right biceps up close to your chin. Hold for twenty seconds. Now do the other arm. This stretches the front and back of the shoulders and many of the rotator muscles used to stabilize lock-offs.

Put your right hand over your left shoulder and reach down your back as far as you can. Put your left hand on your right elbow and push gently to extend the stretch and work the rear deltoid, triceps, and latissimus muscles. Now switch. Avoid the tendency to hold your breath.

Do that same reach over the shoulder, only this time reach up with the other hand and try to shake hands or touch fingers. If you can't touch, work up to it with a towel or a section of rope. Now switch hands. This stretch combines the muscles of the last stretch with those of the front side of the shoulder.

Now for the fingers. Put your right arm straight out in front of you and pull back first one finger, then the next. Gently do it with the palm toward you, then with the palm away from you with fingers over the head. Now the other hand. Don't forget the thumbs. Remember to breathe.

With your palms down, slowly bend your wrists back toward the body and hold. Repeat with the palms up.

Next, the back. Still standing, find a point on the wall behind

Pelvis stretch.

Feet and arms hug the wall in the full-body stretch (*top*). The arms stretch outward (*middle*) and upward (*right*).

you and slowly twist until you can see it. Now gently twist the other way to see it. Keep your hips as stationary as possible.

Now the quads, those strong muscles in the front of your thighs. Sag into one knee, then the other, bending the knee in the same direction you point your toes. Sag lower by pushing your bent leg with your elbow; it's not necessary to go all the way down.

Targeting the pelvis, put your hands on your hips and squat down until your upper leg is parallel to the ground; don't go too far or you can strain your knee. Put your hands over your head, interlocking your fingers, then down to either side, as though pushing against two imaginary walls. Hold this position, concentrating on being solid, like the foundation of a house. Now return to a full standing position and take a few deep breaths.

Now, up against the wall, feet splayed out parallel to the wall, arms spread out and up against the wall, reach out and up, as though extending for holds. Extend to the maximum—feel the stretch. Remember to breathe.

Power

The quest for power haunts climbers and often makes them lose sight of their real goal: to get to the top of the route using only the strength needed for each move—not more, not less.

Three good ways to gain power are by doing specific exercises on a fingerboard, bouldering, and working a hard route.

Using a Fingerboard. Adjusting the duration and intensity for your own fitness level, your fingerboard session might go like this:

1. Warm-up—two-arm pull-ups. Five sets of five to ten repetitions, or two pull-ups, rest, three pull-ups, rest, and so on.
2. Two-arm dead hangs. Hang for ten to thirty seconds on edges ranging in size from 10 (hard) to 20 (medium) to 40 (easy) millimeters.
3. One-arm dead hangs with bungee cords or two-arm hangs with weights. Attach the bungee to the beam and loop it under your foot or attach it to a sling and put your foot into its loop. Put your left foot in the bungee loop if you're working your right arm, and your right foot in the bungee loop if you're working your left arm. Use enough bungees or weight so that you can barely hang for the desired amount of time. Your first session or two will reveal your limits. Try the number of bungees or the amount of weight that allows you to hang for twenty seconds,

The one-arm dead hang. The bungee cord's resistance makes the body's weight easier to lift with one arm.

then rest about three minutes. Adjust the resistance so that you can barely hang for twelve seconds. Rest. Adjust for seven sec-onds. Rest. Adjust for twelve seconds, then twenty seconds. Rest about three minutes between sets. Keep a record of each session not only to show your progress but also to give you a clear idea of how many bungees or how much weight you should use based on your last workout.

Bouldering for Power. Bouldering is probably the most enjoyable way to practice technique and train for power. Your bouldering time will be limited, especially in the beginning, by your raw power and durability of the skin on your fingertips. On an artificial wall at least 6 feet high, arrange the holds to create bouldering circuits of one to five moves on an artificial wall and up to ten on natural rock. Vary the moves and holds.

Boulder for power by working problems at or near your limit. To develop finger power, choose holds you can barely hang on to; to develop arm power, pick large holds that are far apart and don't stress your fingers. Do long reaches and dynos to work the larger muscles in your arms, shoulders, and back. And do traverses, which use different muscles than climbing up and down does.

Working a Hard Route. You can also work power on natural cliffs. Choose a difficult route, one that demands that you work one move at a time or several sections at a time. Called hangdogging, this method enables you to try a variety of techniques while building power. Once you have all the moves worked out, you should be ready to try to link two sections and eventually the entire route.

On an overhanging wall, bolt on holds in a variety of shapes, making sure that they don't stress your fingers or joints. The size of the holds will vary according to your ability and fitness, but they should be large enough to permit you to go up and down without using your feet. Space the big holds far apart and the small edges closer together. A campus board or fingerboard also works well if you vary the position and size of the holds. This is recommended only for experienced climbers.

Work up to five or six dynos in a row at the hardest level possible. Repeat six to ten times and rest to full recovery between sets. For added difficulty, rest two to three minutes between sets. You can also work without using your feet, but you must stay very static to avoid the risk of injury. If you decide to work the descent, be sure to control each movement. Never fall from one hold to another—this is the quickest way to develop tendinitis in the elbow.

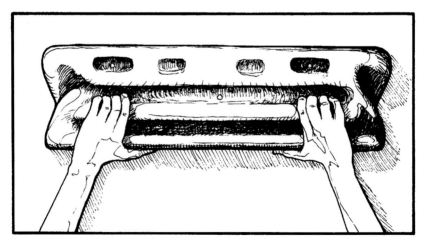

Fingerboards come in all shapes and sizes.

Stamina

Stamina can be worked by choosing a medium-hard route and doing it three times, resting a minute and a half to two minutes between laps. Rest ten minutes, and try it, or another route, three more times.

To help you gauge the difficulty of the route, keep in mind that the optimum sequence should go like this:

First lap: You top out and don't feel too pumped.

Second lap: You finish pumped.

Third lap: You barely make it to the top or fall at the end.

Fourth lap: After a ten-minute rest, you barely make it or fall near the end.

Fifth lap: You fall near the end.

Sixth lap: You fall in the middle.

It is not necessary to finish the route. You should start your one-and-a-half-minute rest after failure.

Volume

Volume is best worked at the end of your training session when you're a little tired. For example, choose five routes that are medium to easy for you when fresh, and do each one with only five minutes of rest in between.

Weight Training

I lift weights, most intently right after the end of the season. It's winter then, and I'm looking to kick back for a while, but I don't want to detrain by doing nothing. So I do low-weight, high-repetition sets, concentrating on cardiovascular fitness.

Sure, I'd rather be outside climbing on the crags than pumping iron. In addition, as I've said, pure strength is no substitute for climbing technique. Still, weight training indirectly helps my technique while it builds strength and endurance and prevents injury. I especially concentrate on muscles that I don't use while climbing, such as pushing muscles.

Climbing maneuvers, such as reaches, stems, high-steps, knee-drops, and cross-throughs, are mechanically disadvantageous to your body, placing enormous pressure on the tendons and ligaments of your joints. A weight-training program strengthens those tendons and ligaments, and also develops the muscles so they can take more of the strain. The most common format for weight training is two days on, one day off, two days on, two days off, with each workout lasting about one and a half to two hours. Avoid working the same muscle groups two days in a row; targeting two muscle groups during a seven-day rotation is fine.

To train endurance, do three to four sets of the following exercises, with twelve to twenty repetitions per set. In between sets, rest for two to three minutes. The ideal weight is one that takes you to exhaustion on the last repetition of each set.

Cable pulls (for the back)
Cable pulls (for the shoulders)
Dumbbell lifts (for the shoulders)
Biceps curls with dumbbells
Pull-downs (for the back)

Consult any basic weight-lifting book or a personal trainer to learn proper body positioning and detailed explanation of these exercises.

To train strength, do four to six sets of each exercise, with six to ten repetitions per set. Again, the weight should be sufficient to exhaust you on the last rep of each set. For both endurance and strength, the weight is too heavy if you cannot execute each repetition with good form.

Hands

Too often when people set out to increase strength, they focus disproportionately on building statuesque biceps. But climbing demands strength from lots of different muscles and joints, including those in the back, shoulders, and hands.

Athletes often take their hands for granted. They spend countless hours exercising the large-muscle groups and improving cardiovascular conditioning, and almost no time developing their hands. For climbers, however, the hands are important, as they are what link us to the rock, and continued stress on unprepared hands and fingers can lead to debilitating injury.

Hands carry out a vast array of functions by way of a network of tendons and muscles stretching from the tips of your fingers to your elbows. The thick forearm muscles control gross grip strength—that's the power you feel from a viselike handshake. The smaller palm muscles at the base of the thumb and fingers are responsible for finer movements, such as feeling for a hold. Called the abductor muscles, they stretch laterally across the hand. If the muscles that control your hands aren't developed well enough to hold up to the demands of a particular activity, the strain will usually be transferred to the tendons. Stretching and strengthening your hands and forearm muscles can help prevent mishaps ranging from minor finger and wrist sprains to dislocations, contusions, tendinitis, and fractures.

In the past, coaches and trainers would address the problem by tossing athletes rubber balls and telling them to squeeze until the cows came home. But squeezing a rubber ball improves only gross grip strength; it doesn't help build fingers that are individually strong, adept, and capable of a full range of motion—the sort of fingers you need for climbing.

There are two basic schools of thought on how to train hands. One argues that the only true way to improve your hands for climbing is to climb; the other says that it's possible to simulate the specific demands of climbing off the wall. Though I agree that the most important exercise for climbers is climbing, there are plenty of useful hand exercises you can do off the wall.

One is to knead, gently and rhythmically, a hunk of Power Putty. This type of elasticized clay is more effective than rubber balls or spring-coil hand grips for working every finger independently. Besides squeezing, you can do the opposite by putting all of your fingers together and sinking them into a flattened putty, then opening your hand. Five to ten minutes daily will work the wrist, palm, and fingers.

Or wrap a thick rubber band around your fingertips and spread your fingers as wide as possible. The band must be taut, so double it if need be. Repeat until your fingers become fatigued, several times daily.

Sink your hand to the wrist in dry sand and try to bend and straighten your fingers quickly. Later, when your fingers are stronger, wet the sand to add resistance.

There are other hand exercisers on the market, ranging from cheap springs with plastic handles to an ergonomically designed gizmo that features individual spring-tension keys for each finger. Originally a rehabilitation device, it is now the hand exerciser of choice for many trainers, coaches, and climbers.

Perhaps the most specific exercises for finger strength is using the training board, or fingerboard.

Free weights are also a good way to strengthen the forearm mus-

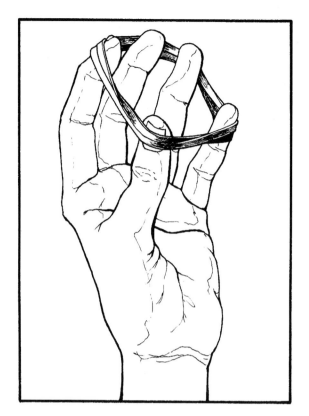

The fingertip rubber band exercise.

cles, which account for about half our grip strength. Using a metal bar or dumbbell of manageable weight, try the following exercises. Be sure to do the warm-up first.

As with all exercise, stay tuned to signs of overuse, such as pains in the wrist. When in doubt, don't be afraid to take a day off.

For Hands. You should warm up the hands, just as you would any other part of the body. With no weight, extend your arms straight out at your sides, then open and close your hands rapidly for about thirty seconds. Spread your fingers as far as you can each time to work the full range of motion. Feel the extensor muscles of the forearm tensing and relaxing, tensing and relaxing.

Wrist Curls. This exercise works the forearms' flexor muscles. Seated with dumbbell in hand, rest your forearm on your thigh or on a table and curl the weight, moving the wrist, not the elbow. Make

Wrist curls.

Reverse wrist curls.

sure your thumb is underneath the weight's bar to better isolate the muscles. Increase your range of motion by bending your wrist as far as you can. Emphasize low-weight, high-repetition sets to improve endurance and avoid injury. Use only as much weight as you can handle for three sets of thirty reps. Work one forearm at a time. Remember to work both sides.

Reverse Curls. I use a bar instead of dumbbells for this exercise. From a standing position, hold the bar in front of your thighs, fingers over the top of the bar, thumbs underneath. Keeping your elbows close to the body and still, lift until your wrists are bent at their maximum. Do three sets of thirty reps with relatively light weights.

Wrist Twists. This exercise isolates the muscles that permit your hand to twist—the supinating and pronating muscles. Weight in hand, rest your upper arm on a table, elbow bent 90 degrees, forearm straight up. Gently torque the wrist back and forth laterally through its full range of motion. Do three sets of fifteen to twenty reps.

Mental Training

You will climb only as high and as well as your mind will let you. In other words, training your mind is every bit as important as training your body. Two areas that I think are especially important are improving your concentration and developing harmony with the climb. I recommend reading a book called *The Mental Athlete,* by Dr. Kaye Porter. Full of valuable advice on mental training and stress management, it's had a positive influence on me.

Concentration is a weak point for many climbers. At inopportune moments, when you should be focusing on the moves before you, your attention may wander to what your belayer is up to, how the climber next to you is doing, or other nonproductive thoughts.

Here's an exercise for improving your concentration: Sit comfortably in a lotus or half-lotus position, and close your eyes. Begin slow, deep, quiet breathing, paying attention to the nuances of each breath. When you feel relaxed, begin counting each of your exhalations. When you reach ten, start over again. If you lose your place or fail to stop at ten, analyze the thoughts that yanked you off track. Then start counting again. Do this for ten-minute stretches, and feel your concentration sharpen.

Here's an exercise that you can do on the wall: On warm-ups and easy routes below your on-sight level, use every hold that you first touch. This exercise, called "the hold you touch is the hold you use," forces you to place each limb softly and precisely only once on each hold, avoiding "touchy feely" climbing. It also forces you to think before you move and develops your powers of visualization.

It's also important to improve your harmony with the climb. Avoid combat metaphors, such as "conquer," "attack," or "fight." Instead, think of the climb as a friendly undertaking, a search for harmony and rhythm. To succeed, you need a solid partnership between yourself and the rock. I look at the climb as a puzzle to be solved. Instead of fighting it, I'm looking for the easiest way to the top, the path of least resistance. I don't want to expend any more energy than I have to.

By diligently working on these mental techniques in training, you will sharpen the tools necessary to succeed in competition, as well as raise your on-sight level and your ability to redpoint a difficult route. The more you practice them, the more you can count on them at crunch time.

Partnerships

Working with a partner can be a great motivator. At its best, a partnership spurs on both parties just the right amount—enough to cause progress, but not so much as to cause injury. When working out with others, you're more likely to experiment with different moves, opening you to new styles and techniques.

Watching another, preferably better, climber is another great way to learn. It helps you improve your ability to analyze other people's techniques, and thus your own. Doing this alone, introspectively, is hard; we lack objectivity and can't see our own bodies, although video review helps climbers develop body awareness.

If you're going to maintain a serious training program, however, you have to be willing to work out by yourself. It's nice to have a partner, but they're not always available or able to perform at your level.

Nutrition

My motto is "everything in moderation." I'm not a vegetarian, and I don't recommend that climbers be vegetarians unless they can't digest meat or have some spiritual or moral reason for not eating it.

I think it's important to maintain a well-rounded diet and a varied menu, paying particular attention to fat and sugar. But I'm not a fanatic about it. Although strength-to-weight ratio is undeniably important to climbers, it would be a mistake to eliminate fat altogether. At 5 feet, 1^1/$_2$ inches and usually about 100 pounds, I'm about average on the women's circuit. A lot of competitors are much skinnier than I am, but I am concerned about the effects of staying really light for a long time. It may help in the short term but hurt in the long term.

When you're training hard, it's vitally important to have good eating habits. I like to keep my weight fairly constant. When I lighten my workout load near a competition, my appetite declines. When I'm away from competition and training hard, I eat more to compensate for those calories burned and to recuperate faster. If I intend to work out in the morning, I have to eat a good dinner the night before, followed by a good breakfast in the morning. I usually divide my workouts around lunch. I don't believe in skipping meals—it leads you to overeating later.

Although I don't count calories, I am conscious of fat. I avoid heavy sauces, fatty processed foods, and cooking with a lot of oil. I get most of my fats from natural foods, such as avocados, nuts, and virgin salad oils. I believe that the less you tamper with food, the greater its nutritional value.

When I do clinics, I often see aspiring climbers arrive with the remains of their pizzas or potato chips—not exactly the diet of champions. Such high-fat foods make your system work overtime, diverting energy that is needed for climbing to digestion. On the other hand, carbohydrates and climbing go together. Fruit, bagels, and PowerBars are easy to carry and to digest. When I'm home for lunch, I'll make pasta or rice, foods that digest quickly enough to allow me to grapple with a boulder problem in a couple of hours. In the evening, I'm more likely to eat a meal higher in protein, because I have all night to digest it.

I try to leave two to three hours after a meal for digestion. If I get to the crag an hour and a half after lunch, I can either delay my start or warm up longer than usual. Because carbohydrates digest so quickly, after two or three hours, I'm starting to get hungry again, so I'll have a PowerBar or a bagel.

Be sure to drink plenty of water. I believe sports drinks are too high in sugar and unnecessary for climbers. Their claim to fame is electrolyte replacement. Electrolytes, such as sodium, potassium, and magnesium, are the minerals in food and drink that are lost in sweat. But climbers are not marathoners. If you are drinking plenty of water and fueling your body with good nutrition, your electrolytes should be just fine.

Scheduling

If you really want to exercise—to train—you will find the time. It's a matter of motivation—no different from finding the time to eat or get dressed. If you stick it at the bottom of your personal priority list, it won't happen. I've heard doctors say that patients who can't find the time to work out invariably change their minds right after their first heart attack.

Schedule your training sessions, just as you'd schedule business meetings or vacations. In fact, think of your workouts as minivacations. Personal preference will dictate whether you work out early, at noon, or late, but the key to staying with it is to make it a commitment and add it to your routine. If you miss a day, you still have a schedule, and you're less likely to abandon the entire program.

Try to be adaptable to changing conditions. For example, if weather, time, or travel makes it temporarily impossible for you to do your favorite workout, find a substitute. Use the gym equipment at your hotel, do floor exercises or isometrics, jump rope, whatever. And with the new climbing gyms cropping up all over the country, chances are a good one is located near you.

− 5 −

Safety

Courage is resistance to fear,
mastery of fear, not absence of fear.

—MARK TWAIN

Safe climbing is a product of your ability to develop good safety skills and your willingness to use them. This includes, among other things, belaying, tying knots, testing knots, using a spotter, and paying attention.

Most climbing errors are caused by loss of concentration. Keep your eyes open and your mind alert at all times to what you and your partner are doing. Climbing can be dangerous, but most problems are caused by climber error and are preventable. No matter how much experience you have, stay with the basics. If you adhere to the script, sport climbing is a lot safer than driving a car, a risk we accept casually.

Knowing the common sport-climbing mistakes is the first step toward eliminating them. Here are a likely top ten:

1. The leader climbs with the rope running behind her leg instead of in front of it. If she falls, the rope can now flip her upside down. Always make sure the rope is running in front of, and preferably to the side of, your legs.

2. The leader forgets to completely tie her knot. This happened to Lynn Hill, so it can happen to you. Intermediate climbers are particularly susceptible to this mistake—they know the right way to do it but forget because it's old hat. The antidote is paying attention, going through your mental checklist, and not skipping steps. Even if you've performed the sequence a hundred times, make sure the rope is fed through the belay device

the right way, make sure the locking carabiner is locked, make sure the harness is double backed, and so forth.

3. The leader expects a belay, but the belayer takes the leader off belay. This is a classic communication problem, rectified by "overcommunicating." For example, if the leader says, "Off," a good belayer will immediately respond with, "I'm going to take you off belay, okay?" The climber will usually respond, "Yes, go ahead," but the first time she screams, "No! Don't take me off!" you'll understand the value of overcommunication. Always tell the leader, "I'm taking you off," and wait for the leader's confirmation, "Yes, take me off," and eye contact, when possible. If she says nothing or you don't understand what she says, ask for clarification.

4. The belayer doesn't catch the leader's fall, resulting in a ground-fall. This is due to lack of attention, lack of anticipation. The belayer should assume the leader is capable of unpredictable behavior at any time. Belaying is life and death, and there should be a minimum of surprises between belayer and climber. The Grigri can help to mitigate the results of such surprises.

5. The leader forgets to double-pass her harness buckle, or ties into the belay loop of her harness. Again, go through your mental checklist each and every time, no matter how much experience you've had.

6. The leader backclips a twisted quickdraw and the rope becomes unclipped.

7. The leader top-ropes off an unsafe anchor. Although this is not a problem in indoor gyms, it can be at the crags.

8. The leader, through inexperience or lack of anticipation, falls poorly, out of control (See chapter 3).

9. The belayer sets up too far away from the first bolt. In the event of a fall, the belayer is dragged toward the wall and the climber does a full plummet. Standing so far away also puts more outward stress on that first bolt.

10. The belayer uses the belay device incorrectly. If you're using a Sticht plate or a figure eight, learn the procedure. In both cases, you're bending the rope to create friction and control the speed of the rope. Better yet, use a Grigri (see chapter 3).

Injuries

Avoiding injury starts with a good warm-up and begins and ends with being smart. Know when to quit. Fatigue is the main criterion. When you get tired and start thrashing about on the route, that's when you become injured. If something doesn't feel right, stop.

The most common affliction, both traumatic and from overuse, is tendinitis, inflammation of the fibrous cords that anchor muscles to bones, characterized by pain, swelling, warmth, and redness. Tendons are especially vulnerable because the force of muscle contractions is transmitted through them. Ironically, people who exercise regularly are more at risk because of the powerful forces transmitted by their well-developed muscles. The increased tension on the tendons causes them to rub against bones, ligaments, and other tendons, resulting in irritation.

Tendinitis can be deceptive. It may hurt at the start of exercise, diminish during exercise, then return sharply once you've finished. For climbers, fingers, elbows, and shoulders are most at risk.

To prevent tendinitis, always begin with a warm-up and stretching, then start your activity slowly and build up gradually. If you develop symptoms of tendinitis, apply heat to vulnerable parts of the body before exercise, ice afterward.

For closed injuries (skin intact), standard therapy includes RICE— rest, ice, compression, and elevation. Either rest or reduce the intensity of the workout. Actually, research suggests that "active rest" is better than a total stoppage. Give yourself at least a day or two to recover. If you don't improve after a few days, rest longer or go to a specialist. I don't recommend a lot of medication because it masks the pain, an important reminder that things are amiss.

Apply ice to the tender area (but not directly to skin, lest it cause frostbite) for up to twenty minutes right after you finish your workout; repeat every two waking hours. Cooling decreases nerve conduction and pain, constricts blood vessels, limits inflammation, and reduces cellular demand for oxygen. Don't exceed the twenty minutes or you can damage skin and nerves.

Avoid using heat, especially at first. It may offer symptomatic relief, but it will increase the inflammation.

Despite fourteen years of climbing and competing and thousands of hours of training, I've never had an overuse or traumatic tendon injury. I did break an ankle once, but that was a freak accident brought on by a combination of extenuating circumstances and my own negligence. It was actually a rest day, but we were doing a photo shoot on an easy boulder problem. Because of the shoot, I had no spotter. I wasn't concentrating, changed my position to vary the photo, and slipped. One foot hit the other foot, and I fell 15 feet onto a rock.

The first X ray missed the break in the ankle, and so I went without a cast. It happened right before the 1995 season, but I could still climb. I finished third in the first event but had to struggle, a sign that something was wrong. In Frankfurt a doctor felt my ankle and declared that it was so hot, it had to be broken. Sure enough it was, as a second X ray showed.

Apart from that, I've had no finger injuries, no tendinitis, no joint problems. I attribute it mostly to the extensive warm-up I do before every workout (see chapter 4), and knowing when to stop.

Partner Safety

Sometimes you do everything correctly, safely, and yet you're endangered because your partner made an error. Get to know your partner and maintain good communication with him or her at all times. Don't be afraid to ask the important questions, such as "Have you ever belayed someone while leading?" and "Have you ever spotted someone?"

Spotting. People tend to think of bouldering as a solitary pursuit, but there are times when you need someone else as a spotter to cushion your falls.

If there's any chance of a long or awkward fall, why land on your feet and jar your back time after time if you can take the pressure off with a spotter or added mattress? I use one whenever my instinct tells me I don't want to fall by myself.

Spotting is a skill, and as a boulderer you have every right to insist that it be done correctly. On the other hand, if your partner's not used to spotting, or you're using your twelve-year-old nephew, don't count on him. Know the risks.

Spotter and climber must work together as a team. The climber should fall one way when alone and quite another way when using a spotter. When you're alone, you need to scope out your boundaries and figure where you want to land. Try to land on your feet, limbs relaxed, knees bent to distribute the shock of the fall. With no spotter, your arms may fly out for balance. With a spotter, however, flailing arms are dangerous, so you must learn to fall relaxed and linear.

As a spotter, stay alert and never assume the climber won't fall. Closely follow the climber, with your eyes focused on the hips and your hands and arms ready. The hips are the easiest place to grab somebody who's falling. Too many spotters are zeroed in on the hands, looking for the telltale slip. Another common error is being way off line, say directly below a left-leaning climber. Try to calculate which direction the climber will fall, and position yourself where you can do the most good. On a fall, catch the climber by the hips or waist and guide him to the ground, protecting his head and back from hitting anything. Protect yourself as well, keeping your head back so that you don't get smacked in the face and your thumbs tucked in to avoid a sprain.

In 1993 the British Orthopaedic Association announced that climbing injuries on artificial walls occurred, on average, only once every 18,600 visits, making sport climbing safer than many sports, including squash or soccer.

Belaying. Belaying (see chapter 3) is a life-and-death skill. For maximum safety, observe the following dos and don'ts:

- Never remove the brake hand.
- If you're not sure of the route's length, tie a knot at the end of the rope so as not to drop the climber.
- Tie down the belayer if he is much lighter than the climber or if there is a risk of a groundfall.
- If you're unfamiliar with belay anchors and knots used for belaying, be sure to consult a basic book on the subject or ask an experienced climber.

Dynamic Belaying. When a climber falls, the novice belayer's natural tendency is to take in rope. But as we now know, that actually increases the impact of the fall, effectively sucking the climber into the rock. The result, too often, is a broken ankle or a smashed head.

The correct alternative, called *dynamic belaying*, requires the belayer to feed out a little rope to mitigate the fall. In this skill, the body's weight is placed on a forward, bent leg while the back leg stays relaxed. This position makes you ready to fall forward with the falling climber, effectively reducing the impact of the climber's fall. This is an advanced skill that takes concentration and practice, but it's worth the effort.

Knots. Two common knots in sport climbing are the figure eight and the bowline. The advantage of knots over more permanent ways of joining ropes and cords together—like sewn slings—is that knots can be easily untied and retied. The disadvantage is that they weaken the rope, so check regularly for wear.

Figure-Eight Knot. A figure-eight knot can be used as a stopper knot on the end of a rope, for tying two ropes together, or for tying into your climbing harness.

1. Make a bight, passing the loop behind the static part of the rope.
2. Pass the end over the near side and through the loop.
3. Draw the knot tight.
4. Finish off with a half hitch.

Bowline knot. A bowline can also be used to tie your rope to your climbing harness. Avoid a three-way pull on this knot, as that may untie it.

1. Make a loop in the rope.
2. Pass the tail up through the loop.
3. Pass the tail around behind the static rope and back through the loop.
4. Complete the loop by tying a half hitch on the end; this will prevent slipping.

For more comprehensive information on common knots used in climbing, consult such a basic rock climbing book as *Rock Climbing Basics*, by Turlough Johnston & Madeleine Hallden, published by Stackpole Books, 1995.

– 6 –

Competition

*Success seems to be largely a matter of hanging on
after others have let go.*

—WILLIAM FEATHER

To speak of competitive sport climbing is to speak of indoor events on artificial walls with routes that are altered for maximum competitive value. As competitors progress from the qualifiers to the quarterfinals to the semifinals to the finals, the routes become increasingly more difficult. Routes are customized for men and for women.

Sport-climbing competitions range from regional events to national and world championships. Regional events are usually held in climbing gyms; World Cup events and other major competitions are held in big halls or auditoriums, where 50- to 75-foot walls are built specially for the events and torn down when they're over.

Most competitions are on-sight events in which competitors try to reach the top of a wall on the first try with no prior knowledge of the moves other than what they can glean from a short observation period, usually six minutes. Except for that observation period, climbers are kept in isolation until they attempt the route.

A fall determines a competitor's high point and thus his or her placement in the event. A competition might start with fifty women and seventy-five men, then get cut to sixteen women and twenty-six men for the semis, and eight women and eight men for the finals. In the finals, ideally only one climber reaches the top while the others fall off somewhere below. If two or more finalists reach the top, they square off in a superfinal.

Observation Period

If the event is scheduled to start at 9:30, then all of the competitors are led out at around 9:20 for the six-minute observation period. All of the quickdraws are already in place, and the course setter or representative is there to show the competitors the general line of the route.

I make the most of the observation period, scrutinizing the route from bottom to top, all thirty to fifty moves. I look at the handholds and footholds and try to imagine each sequence, committing as much detail to memory as possible. Experience, of course, makes that easier. Novices might look at only the first ten moves of the route, partly because that's all they can store away and partly because they can't imagine climbing higher than that. After countless observation periods, I am usually able to remember every single move from bottom to top.

The sequence I follow during the observation period goes like this:

1. I inspect the entire route, following the general line.
2. In my mind, I begin the route from the first hold, and I pantomime the movements. I consider foot placements and look for the best positions from which to clip. During this phase, I don't spend much time on the complicated sections.
3. Now I return to the complicated sections and try to find an obvious sequence; if not, I imagine two solutions.
4. I look for rest positions, if any.
5. If time remains, I restudy the first 15 feet.

As I study the route, the audio track of my mental film clip might sound something like this: "Blue crimper, right hand, to undercling left hand . . . important foothold out right . . . big move to red hold . . . clip. Shake right hand, left hand to two-finger pocket . . ."

Practice this type of observation in your training. Carefully study routes for about six minutes, trying to stimulate and enhance your powers of recall. As you climb, check your accuracy.

Isolation

One of the truly unique features of climbing competitions is that often you don't get to see your main rivals climb. Competitive sport climbers spend a lot of time in what's called the *isolation zone*. Isolation is a necessary evil in competition climbing; without it, later climbers can obtain too much information from earlier climbers, giving them an unfair advantage.

If my draw is twenty-second, I might spend three hours in isolation, waiting for my turn to climb. How I use that time can spell the difference between climbing well and climbing poorly. Everyone has a different way of coping and preparing. I warm up, relax, rememorize the route, talk to my friends, read, and stretch. Others play basketball or meditate.

After the observation period, I take the first few minutes in isolation to sit quietly and run my mental film clip, revisiting the route in as much detail as possible. This is a very focused time for me, during which I avoid conversation. After a few minutes, though, when I feel I have the route firmly in my mind, I'll talk to my friends. We compare notes, review what we saw, discuss problems and possible solutions: "Remember that section at the roof where you grab the red hold with the right hand? Well, do you think you're going to cross there or are you going to go out to that hold on the left and do a heel hook?"

I hold back very few secrets from my competitors. I want the sport

to remain friendly. The top women are all good friends, all rooting for each other, all sharing with each other. I want my competitors to climb their very best, and I must believe that I'm the strongest that day. If I give others a heel hook on the twentieth move, then everyone's going

Although competitions last all day, each climber spends only a few minutes on the wall.

to be climbing at their maximum. I don't want to win because others climb badly. I remain confident that if I am well trained and climbing my best, I can win even if everyone else climbs well, too.

The exchange is by no means one-sided. I give information, I get information. We're all kind of stepping on each other's shoulders to get up higher, and by pooling information and support we all progress. I don't really like sharing information with someone who's making no effort to improve, but the best ones aren't like that. And even when I'm approached by someone who's scoped out only the first ten moves, asking me what I'm going to do on the roof, I tell her. I figure if we all have the same information, the best will win.

Competition Day Schedule

In the following example, my climbing order is twenty-two. Figuring seven minutes per climber tells me that my starting time will be about two and a half hours after the first climber goes off. I pace myself accordingly:

7:30   Run, stretch, and generally wake up
8:15   Breakfast
8:45   Enter isolation
9:00   Easy climbing as a warm-up
9:20   Observation of route
9:30   Competition begins and I continue to warm up
11:20   Finish warm-up
11:30   Clean climbing shoes, change clothes
12:00   Climb

The Mental Game

The mental aspect of sport climbing may be the most important part; it underlies everything, makes it all possible. You work a route, know its degree of difficulty, know you can do the moves, and yet something from the neck up keeps you from doing them. A strong body working with a flabby mind at the controls is a recipe for disaster—or at least failure.

The keys to winning the mental game are focus and fun. Focus, or concentration, is at the heart of athletic success, and nowhere is it more important than in climbing. One way of enhancing concentration is through the process of visualization, a type of mental rehearsal in which you conjure up detailed visions of the activity before you do it.

I use visualization a lot after the observation period, though not necessarily for every event—it's tiring and you can overtrain the mind just as you can the body. When I look at a route, I spend the entire six minutes in deep concentration, assimilating as much information as possible. I try to read the route and remember details. I see myself doing it, move by move. Then, when I'm back in isolation, instead of chatting or playing basketball or soccer, I spend the first few minutes rolling my mental tape over and over.

I figure if I can recall, and store in my memory, 80 percent of the information I've absorbed, that's 80 percent less climbing time I have to spend weighting my arms looking for the moves.

Another way to enhance concentration is through positive association. Start this before you even get on the wall. As you lace your climbing shoes, think to yourself: "I am lacing my shoes well." And if something goes wrong—your shoelace breaks—find a way to turn it into a positive: "Boy, I must really be strong today."

As other negatives surface, meet them head on and change them. Make a mental list of the things that bother you. This allows you to face your fears and overcome mental blocks. For example:

1. I am afraid of falling.
2. She is stronger than I am.
3. I don't feel in shape.

Now consider the consequences of each problem.

1. If I fall—and that's unlikely—the fall will be safe. So what will happen? I'll be unhappy, but otherwise the consequences will not be dramatic. Therefore, the fear of falling is unjustified.
2. Okay, maybe she is stronger than I am, but who really knows? She has nothing to do with my performance. I am here to enjoy the route created by the route setters. I am prepared to climb well, and to find harmony on the route.
3. Telling myself that I feel out of shape will not help me climb better; on the other hand, to blindly assert the opposite, if it's untrue, would be self-deception. I must focus my concentration even more to assure that I climb to the limits of my strength. Today it is most important that I do each move using the least energy possible. I want to rest efficiently but not hesitate so as to cause unnecessary pump.

Good concentration does not preclude having fun. The more you

Competitive success requires a balance between seriousness and levity.

can make competition seem like climbing at your favorite crag, the better. And the more uptight you are, the worse the results. Try to relax the parts of your body you're not using.

Competitive success, then, requires a delicate balance of seriousness and levity. You have to be serious to be successful, but that doesn't mean you can't enjoy yourself. If you are hard-wired for competition, you can manage both simultaneously.

So much of climbing is learning to deal with failure. Malcolm Forbes once said that "failure is success if we learn from it," and that's certainly true in climbing. You have to be able to pick yourself up after a fall and go at it again and again. If you're unwilling to fall or take risks, you simply can't progress. Anyone can stick with it when everything is going well; the difference between great and so-so is often how you respond when things are falling apart. You may suffer through a slump that lasts a month, but perseverance through adversity like that can take you to new heights.

Stress Management

Elite competition climbers perform in front of thousands of spectators. Such attention can get the heart pumping, the adrenaline flowing.

Beginners may experience a similar biochemical rush in an empty gym. Whether those changes affect your performance depends on how you handle stress.

The first step is recognizing that you're stressed. Say it hits you when you're putting on your shoes. Stop right there and take a few minutes to calm down. My inner dialogue might go like this: "Okay, I'm stressed because it's important to me. That's fine, but if I'm too stressed, my performance will suffer. How to control it and relax? Good breathing, relaxation, positive thoughts. My positive thought is that I am going to concentrate on good climbing and remember that I am here to have fun and there is nothing to lose."

Up on the wall, I want to continue to use those same tools that have long worked for me. My inner dialogue includes reminders to be precise and smart—and to breathe.

The mental and emotional strength necessary to prepare for competition comes with experience. I credit my win in the 1989 Leeds World Cup, my first major competition, to a good attitude and determination. To win over and over again takes experience.

So get out there and get experience. Almost all climbing gyms have classes, leagues, and regional competitions for both children and adults. Sport climbing offers something for everyone.

For information about upcoming events, contact your local climbing gym, or the American Sport Climbers Federation, 35 Greenfield Dr., Moraga, CA 94556, telephone: (510) 376-1640.

Course setter Christian Griffith says his goal in creating a course is "an extreme sequence of moves that continually get harder and harder, but not too hard. I try to make it fair for everyone, to complement both short and tall climbers. My goal is to make climbing a dance, a dance of difficulty and tenacity."

– 7 –

Official Climbing Competition Rules

The rules of the American Sport Climbers Federation are always under review. This version is reviewed as of February 6, 1996. Keep in mind that the sport is young and that the rules will continue to evolve as we learn more. The rules that follow have been edited for style.

Rule 1. Out of Bounds
The entire surface of the climbing wall is permitted for climbing, with the following exceptions:
   a) top and side edges (which may be marked with colored tape)
   b) any object marked as out of bounds or off-route (again, with distinctly colored tape)
   c) any bolt, bolt hanger, or quickdraw
   d) an adjacent wall that might be out of bounds (marked with continuous colored tape)

Rule 2. Observation
   a) Before the start of the heat, all competitors may study the route for an amount of time set by the ASCF chief judge. In the case of multi-route rounds or superfinals, the chief judge may elect to have no observation time.
   b) Prior to the observation time, the route must be finished and the quickdraws in place.
   c) During observation time, competitors must stay within the observation zone, which is, if necessary, clearly marked.

d) Only competitors may enter the observation zone during the designated observation period. Coaches, managers, and others who accompany climbers to the isolation zone must remain in isolation during the observation period.

e) No electronic devices or recording equipment may be used during the observation period.

Rule 3. Timing

a) A time limit shall be set for each route by the ASCF chief judge. For single-route rounds, the climber must be tied in before the clock starts.

b) The clock starts when the competitor, moving from the transit zone, crosses a designated line. At this point, the climber has forty seconds to start the climb.

c) If the climbing time elapses, the chief route judge shall stop the competitor and measure the farthest hold touched or held.

d) Either the timing judge or the chief route judge is responsible for calling out the last minute and the last ten seconds of the climber's time, as well as the remaining time at the climber's request. It is not required that the remaining time be available on multi-route rounds.

e) With the exception of d) above, once the climber has received final instructions and signaled his readiness to start, no further instructions or information shall be given to the climber by any official.

Rule 4. Starting Positions

Rules regarding starting positions may be set by the chief judge. In a heat where the starting position is marked, each climber is allowed one misstart. The climber must restart immediately. If the same climber misstarts again, he/she shall not be scored for that route.

Rule 5

Falls to the ground or on an edge must not be possible. For that reason, the first belay point may be preclipped. All subsequent clip-in points must be placed a safe distance apart. It must be ensured that a competitor's fall does not affect another competitor on an adjoining route.

Rule 6

The belayer shall leave an appropriate amount of slack rope at all times. Any tension on the rope may end the competitor's attempt.

Rule 7

A competitor may climb downward at any time but may not return to the ground. "Returning to the ground" is to be interpreted as any part of the climber's body weighting the ground/floor after both feet have left the ground/floor and the climber has begun his/her climb.

Rule 8. Equipment

a) Each competitor may use whatever legal technical equipment and materials he/she chooses, such as climbing shoes, seat harnesses, chalk bag, helmet. All new equipment developments are subject to the authorization of the ASCF. The use of a commercially produced seat harness with leg loops is compulsory. Equipment and materials shall comply with UIAA safety specifications unless otherwise specified under a special exception granted by the ASCF, which may delegate its power to the ASCF chief judge.

b) The competitors shall use a single rope supplied by the organizer. Minimum diameters for lead-type competition ropes are: 10 mm for adults and 9.8 for juniors. The frequency with which ropes are replaced shall be decided by the route judge.

Rule 9. Technical Incidents

A technical incident will be dealt with as follows:

a) If a competitor wishes and is still in regular position, he/she can continue climbing unless the route judge is calling the technical incident. In either case, no further appeal is possible.

b) A climber may indicate the occurrence of a technical incident. If the climber wishes to claim a technical incident, he/she must do so immediately. If a climber's attempt ends because of a claimed technical incident, the route judge will decide the case.

c) If the competitor's attempt ends, or is stopped by the route judge due to an apparent technical incident, the competitor is immediately taken to a separate isolation zone.

d) The competitor must decide immediately when to start his/her second attempt, but it must occur no later than after the fifth fol-lowing competitor. The climber shall be permitted a minimum recuperation time of fifteen minutes between attempts.

e) In the event of a second attempt, the route judge will record the best attempt for the climber's final result.

f) If a hold or a part of the climbing structure breaks, the route judge and the route setter will try to repair the route as best they can. If this is impossible, the heat may be continued or canceled without the right of appeal.

Rule 10. Disqualification

The Competition Climbing Committee of the ASCF reserves the right to exclude from participation in future ASCF-sanctioned competitions, with or without restriction, all competitors who refuse to follow a judge's instructions or decisions, or whose behavior is deemed unsportsmanlike or adverse to the best interest of the sport. This pro-hibition could include representatives of the offending climber, such as coaches, managers, or family.

Rule 11

a) When ascending, a competitor shall clip all belay points in order.

b) A competitor shall clip before his/her entire body has moved beyond the lowest carabiner of a belay point. Any violation of this rule shall result in the climb being stopped and a measure-ment taken. However, the route judge, believing that a violation is about to occur, may inform the competitor. Failure to do so shall not be grounds for protest or appeal.

Rule 12

A competitor's climb is finished in the event of the following viola-tions:

a) falling;

b) exceeding the permitted climbing time;

c) climbing on a prohibited part of the wall;

d) failing to clip all belay points in order;

e) returning to the ground;

f) using artificial aid.

Rule 13

In the event of a fall or an ordered stop, the furthest hold held along the route will be measured.

a) In the case of two or more competitors holding equal holds, the competitor who makes useful movement off the hold will be considered better.

b) In the case of two or more competitors making useful movement off the same hold, the competitor who touches the usable part of the hold farther along the route will be considered better.

c) If, after taking into account a) and b) above, two or more competitors are still tied, the competitor who has clipped the quickdraw farthest along the route will be considered better.

Notes to Rule 13

- *Holds* and *usable parts of holds* are those considered as such by the route judge or points successfully used by any competitor during the heat. If a competitor touches a point devoid of holds, this point will not be counted.
- *Held a hold* will be determined by the route judge. This might be holding the hold in control or holding it for three or more seconds.
- Moves off of (useful movement) is a movement by the competitor, as determined by the route judge, after the competitor has definitely held the hold.

Rule 14

The following violations may, if intentional, result in the disqualification of the competitor, with loss of points and prize money. Unintentional violation shall result in disqualification without loss of points and prize money. Decisions regarding intent shall be made by the chief judge.

a) Gathering information about the climbing route in excess of the time permitted.

b) Observing the route from outside the marked observation zone during the official observation period.

c) Failure to return to the isolation zone after the route observation period.

d) Failure to be completely equipped when reporting to the start of the route.

e) Use of prohibited or substandard equipment.

f) Unroping after being called to start, except as ordered by the route judge.

g) Unauthorized entry of the isolation zone.

h) Arrival at the warm-up or transit zones after the prescribed time.

i) Refusal to follow the instructions of the supervisory staff in the waiting, isolation, or transit zones.

j) Abusive or insulting comments or behavior, or physical assaults of staff, judges, supervisory staff, ASCF delegates, organizers, media, team captains, or other participants in the competition or audience.

k) Interfering or otherwise bothering another competitor during that competitor's climbing attempt.

l) Refusal to participate in any official ceremonies that are agreed upon by the organizer and officials.

m) Refusal to observe the instructions or decisions of the officials.

Rule 15. Appeals

All competitors have the right to appeal the decisions of judges.

a) A fee of $10 must accompany each written appeal. Fees will be refunded if the appeal is upheld.

b) Appeals due to a technical incident must be lodged with the route judge immediately following the incident. These appeals are verbal and will be answered immediately by the route judge.

c) Appeals of a decision by a route judge must be presented in writing to the ASCF chief judge by the competitor or representative within thirty minutes after the announcement of the judge's decision. The ASCF chief judge will respond in writing to the appeal within one hour of receiving it.

Note: Judges' calls made during a competitor's climbing attempt must be called immediately. The competitor cannot protest or appeal such a call except on the basis of a misinterpretation of a rule by the judge.

National final rounds shall have three route judges per route.

d) Appeals regarding results, either of a heat or a final competition, must be lodged in writing with the ASCF chief judge by the competitor or representative within one hour after the announcement of the official results. The ASCF chief judge will respond to such appeals within twenty-four hours or prior to the start of the following heat, whichever comes first.

e) No appeal filed after the prescribed deadlines will be considered.

f) All official results posted by the ASCF chief judge that are in accordance with the prescribed deadlines are final, regardless of the outcome of grievances filed according to Rule 16.

Rule 16. Grievances

a) Grievances by a competitor may be lodged in writing with the ASCF Competitions Committee up to two weeks after the official closing of the event.

b) The ASCF Competitions Committee will respond in writing directly to the grievant no more than thirty days after receiving the written grievance.

c) No grievance that is filed after the prescribed deadline will be considered.

Rule 17

Whenever the organizing committee is obliged to run the competitors on two separate routes in a single round, the field must be divided equally according to the most recent ASCF-approved ranking list. Unranked competitors are drawn and placed randomly or at the discretion of the organizer and chief judge.

Rule 18

a) In all national-level events, the final and superfinal rounds shall be climbed on lead, with belay from below.

b) A route shall be considered successfully completed if it is climbed according to the rules and when the final quickdraw has been clipped by the competitor from a "regular position." It is not allowed to hold the final quickdraw before it is clipped.

Rule 19

In the case of on-sight competitions:

a) Before the heat, competitors must have no knowledge of their route except what they obtain during the official observation period. Obtaining information about the route(s) outside isolation from staff, friends, media, etc. may lead to disqualification.

b) Competitors must register and enter the isolation zone before the specified time of closing. Only persons authorized by the ASCF chief judge may enter the isolation zone. Managers, coaches, and others who accompany climbers into isolation must abide by the same rules that govern climbers in isolation. Once they leave the isolation zone, they will not, under any conditions, be allowed to reenter.

c) Even after the official closing of the isolation zone, the ASCF chief judge may allow others, such as reporters or photographers, into the isolation zone with an official escort, taking care that the competitors are not disturbed and the isolation rules are not violated.

d) While one competitor is climbing, the next competitor shall be led into the transit zone, where his/her equipment and materials shall be inspected. The competitor shall have his/her shoes on and be ready to go immediately to the climbing wall when called by the route judge. Competitors shall not be able to watch the competition from the transit zone.

e) If a competitor is not ready to go to the start of the climb when called from the transit zone, his/her climbing time may be started at the discretion of the route judge.

f) The following areas, as well as additional areas marked as ISO zones, are all subject to the rules regarding isolation.
   1. Waiting/warm-up areas (primary isolation zone)
   2. Transition zones
   3. Observation zones
   4. Climbing arena (may be same as observation zone)

Rule 20

a) Worked routes: After discussions with the route judge, the ASCF chief judge will decide the duration, timetable, and methods of training permitted each competitor.

b) The judges will supervise the training period and ensure that no competitor exceeds his/her allotted time.

Rule 21

a) The number of competitors in each round of competition shall be determined, in accordance with the regulations, by the ASCF chief judge and communicated to the participants before the start of the heats.

b) The Nationals shall consist of three rounds. No more than two routes shall be used in the qualifier and the semifinals, and no more than one route in the finals. The number of competitors passing into the semis and finals are as follows:

Semis: twenty-five men and fifteen women

Finals: ten men and seven women

Rule 22

a) Climbers will qualify for the next heat based on the quota and the rankings of the previous competition.

b) If, because of ties, the fixed quota is exceeded, a "floating quota" will be used to determine which climbers advance to the next level.

c) In the case described above, either all or none of the tied competitors will move on. The number nearest the fixed quota will be taken. When taking none and taking all are both the same distance from the fixed quota, no climbers shall advance, except that there shall be a minimum of six for the men's final and four for the women's final in a national-level competition (semis: seventeen men and ten women).

d) If the quota is exceeded by tied climbers who competed on separate routes in an earlier round, the tie may not be broken by considering the results of that previous round.

Rule 23

a) After each round of the competition, the competitors are ranked.

b) If there are ties after the semifinal and final rounds, the results of previous rounds will be used to break the ties and determine final placement.

c) In the case described above, the most recent round has the higher value.

d) Results of a qualifying round bypassed by prequalified climbers shall not be used to break ties or stay within a quota.

Rule 24

a) A superfinal is held if there is a tie in the finals for first place, after considering the results of the previous rounds.

b) If there is a tie in the superfinal, the competition shall end in a first-place tie.

Rule 25

Video is not permitted for the purpose of deciding an appeal of a route judge's call. Video may be used in cases where the route judge and chief judge have a special reason to review a certain climber's attempt. Review of video for judging decisions will be solely at the discretion of the route and chief judges.

Refer questions to:

Head of ASCF judges	ASCF Executive Director
Jim Link	Hans Florine
12404 Kingsley	35 Greenfield Dr.
Louisville, KY 40229	Moraga, CA 94556
(502) 957-4486	(510) 376-1640

If you plan to host your own sport climbing event, contact Hans Florine for the most accurate, up-to-date information on rules.

Glossary

abseil: see *rappel.*

accessory cord: thin rope, from 3 to 8 millimeters, often used for making slings, or runners.

active rope: the length of rope between a moving climber and the belayer.

anchor: the point at which a fixed rope, a rappel rope, or a belay is secured to rock, snow, or ice by any of various means.

approach: the distance a climber must hike from the car to the start of the climb. An approach may take anywhere from a few minutes to several days.

arête: a narrow, serrated ridge, usually separating two glacial valleys or adjacent cirques. Also called a *knife edge.*

belay: to tend the climbing rope, ready to immediately put enough friction on the rope to hold the climber in case of a fall. Friction is generated by the rope passing around the belayer's body or through a belay device.

Belaying is the primary safeguard in climbing, and its practice is universal. *Belay* also refers to the entire system set up to make belaying possible, including the anchor that holds the belayer in place.

belay device: any of numerous small metal gadgets that force a bend in the climbing rope, creating enough friction to enable a belayer to hold a fall. See also *descender, figure-eight descender,* and *Grigri.*

bight: a loop of rope.

biner (pronounced "beaner"): slang for *carabiner.*

body belay: see *waist belay.*

body rappel: method of descending in which a climber threads an anchored climbing rope between his legs, returns it to the front of his body, then wraps it over a shoulder and holds it behind him with one hand.

bolt: a thin metal rod that is hammered into a predrilled hole in the rock to serve as a multidirectional anchor. Bolts, ranging in size from $1/4$- to $1/2$-inch, were originally used to protect free climbers on otherwise unprotectable routes and to piece together crack systems on longer climbs. Because they are left in place for subsequent climbers to use, bolts remain controversial.

bolt hanger: a metal piece that is attached to the bolt, allowing a carabiner to be clipped to the bolt.

bombproof: said of a hold or belay that will not fail, regardless of how much weight or force is put on it.

bucket: a large bombproof hold.

bulge: a small overhang.

buttress: a section of a mountain or cliff standing out from the rest, often flanked on both sides by gullies or couloirs; somewhat wider than an arête.

carabiner: an oval or D-shaped metal snap-link about 3 inches long in the shape of a giant safety pin. Capable of holding a ton or more, carabiners are used for attaching the rope to anchors in rock or snow.

chest harness: a harness used in conjunction with a waist harness to attach a climber to the rope. Also great for children.

chock: a rock wedged in a crack or behind a flake, around which a runner can be threaded and then clipped to a rope for an anchor point. Before artificial chocks, British climbers used to carry pebbles to place in cracks; later they used hexagonal machine nuts found on railroad tracks. Today there are two basic types of chocks: wedges and hexes. Also called a *chockstone.*

classic routes: sport climbs that have special character, historical interest, great difficulty, popularity, or a combination of these.

cleaning the pitch: removing all the protection hardware placed by the leader.

cliff: a smooth, steep face of rock.

clip in: to attach oneself to the rock by means of a carabiner snapped onto an anchor.

clove hitch: one of the two main knots (the other is the figure eight) used in the ropework system.

coiling: the various methods of looping and tying a rope so that it can be carried, all requiring a certain amount of skill to avoid kinking.

corner: a junction of two planes of rock, approximately at right angles.

crack: a gap or fracture in the rock, varying in width from a thin seam to a wide chimney.

crag: a low cliff, one or two pitches high.

crux: the most difficult part of a pitch or climb (though some climbs have more than one crux).

daypack: a medium-size soft pack, favored by day hikers, for carrying food, water, and other supplies; bigger than a fanny pack, smaller than a backpack.

dehydration: a depletion of body fluids that can hinder the body's ability to regulate its own temperature. One can become dehydrated during climbing if the fluids lost from perspiration and respiration are not replaced by drinking water. Chronic dehydration lowers a climber's tolerance to fatigue, reduces his ability to sweat, elevates his rectal temperature, and increases the stress on his circulatory system. In general, a loss of 2 percent or more of one's body weight by sweating affects performance; a loss of 5 to 6 percent affects health.

descender: a friction device used for descending ropes (rappelling). The most common is the figure eight; others include the carabiner brake and the Grigri. Also known as a *rappel device.*

dihedral: a high-angled inside corner where two rock planes intersect; shaped like an open book. (Contrasted with *outside corner.*)

direct: the most direct way up a route or climb, usually the way water would take to fall down the rock. The direct tends to be steeper and more difficult than ordinary routes.

double dyno: to let go of both hands at the same time and catch the next two holds high up.

down and out: the correct position of a carabiner gate when it is connected to an anchor.

dyno: a technique for reaching holds that seem just beyond the climber's grasp. The climber throws upward or diagonally with a precise timing, using his legs and one or both arms to dynamically (not statically) fly up to the next hold, which is usually far away.

edging: using the sides of climbing boots to stand on thin rock ledges.

expansion bolt: a bolt that expands and locks when screwed into a prebored hole in the rock. Used when a rock lacks cracks into which a piton or nut can be inserted. Bolts provide the safest protection, but they alter the rock and change the character and degree of difficulty of a climb.

exposed: said of a climber's route that is steep and hard with a big drop below it.

exposure: a long drop beneath a climber's feet; what one confronts to the max when climbing a sheer face like El Capitan.

face: a wall of rock steeper than 60 degrees.

fall factor: a numerical value indicating the severity of a fall. If protection holds, the most serious fall has a value of 2, and most climbing falls are between .5 and 1. Calculate the fall factor by dividing the distance of the fall by the length of rope between you and your belayer.

figure-eight descender: a metal rappelling device in the shape of the numeral 8. One hole is used to attach the device to a harness with a carabiner; a rope is passed through the other hole to provide friction for the descent.

figure-eight knot: one of the two main knots (the other is the clove hitch) used in the ropework system.

finger crack: a crack so thin that only a climber's fingers will fit into it.

first ascent: the first time a route has been climbed.

fist crack: a crack the size of a fist.

fist jam: a secure and painful (for the beginner) way of finding a purchase on a rock. In a fist jam, the climber shoves his hand into a gap in the rock and makes a fist, swelling the hand for use as an anchor point.

fixed protection: anchors, such as bolts or pitons, that are permanently placed in the rock.

fixed rope: a rope that a climber has anchored and left in place after a pitch is climbed so that climbers can ascend and descend at will. Most expedition climbing uses fixed ropes to facilitate load carrying and fast retreat over dangerous terrain.

flake: a thin, partly detached leaf of rock. Also means to prepare a rope so that it won't tangle when you are using it.

flapper: torn skin on the hand—the kind that flaps.

flaring crack: a crack with sides that flare out.

flash: to climb a route the first time, without falling or hanging from the rope, after having seen someone else climb the route or being given information about its moves.

fracture: a break in a rock caused by intense applied pressure.

free climbing: climbing in which natural handholds and footholds are used. Hardware is used only for protection and not for support or progress. (Contrasted with *aid climbing*.)

free soloing: climbing done without ropes, hardware, or a partner.

friction climbing: ascending slabs using friction between shoes and rock or hands and rock, instead of distinct holds.

Friend: an active (spring-loaded) camming device inserted into a crack as an anchor point. Designed and marketed by Ray Jardine in 1978, the Friend was a major breakthrough because it allowed climbers to pro-

tect roofs and parallel cracks with minimal time spent making the placement.

frost wedging: the opening and widening of a crack by the repeated freezing and thawing of ice in the crack.

glacis: an easy-angled slab of rock between horizontal and 30 degrees. A slab is steeper, and a wall steeper yet.

Grigri: a self-locking belay device with an integral security system that locks on to the climber's rope when the rope is pulled sharply. When movement is slow, the rope runs freely through the device; when shock load is reached, the Grigri locks, jamming the rope to a stop.

gorge: a deep, narrow valley with very steep sides.

groove: a shallow, vertical crack.

gully: steep-sided rift or chasm, deep and wide enough to walk inside.

hangdogging: hanging on a rope, usually after a fall or while working a hard route.

hanging belay: a belay station on vertical rock that offers no ledge for support.

harness: a contraption worn around the shoulders or waist, usually made of wide tape, and offering convenient loops through which to clip a climber's rope and gear. If a climber falls while roped onto a harness, the shock load is distributed over a wide area. The climber also has a better chance of remaining in an upright position, lowering the risk of head meeting rock.

headlamp: a light that is mounted on a climber's helmet or headband.

headwall: the sheerest, often most difficult section of a cliff or mountain, usually its uppermost.

helmet: a hard shell that a climber wears to protect his head from falling rock.

hip belay: see *waist belay*.

hold: a protrusion or indentation in the rock that a climber can grasp with fingers (handhold) or stand on (foothold).

horn: a protruding piece of rock over which a sling can be hung for an anchor.

impact force: the tug a falling climber feels from the rope as it stops a fall.

inactive rope: rope between any two climbers who are not moving.

jam crack: a gap in a rock that offers inadequate handholds but is wide enough for the climber to find purchase by inserting fingers, hand, fist, or feet.

jamming: wedging fingers, hand, fist, or feet into a crack to create an anchor point.

jug: a large, indented hold; a bucket.

kernmantle: standard climbing rope in which a core (kern), constructed of one or more braided units, is protected by an outer braided sheath (mantle).

knife edge: see *arête*.

knoll: a small, rounded hill or mound.

laybacking, or liebacking: grabbing a vertical edge, often a flake of rock, then pulling with hands, pushing with feet, and walking the feet up almost alongside the hands. It is a strenuous but useful technique for arêtes, corners with cracks, and cracks offset in walls.

lead, or leader: the first climber in a party of roped climbers.

leader fall: a fall taken by the lead climber. The leader will fall double whatever the distance is to the closest protection.

leading through: said of a second climber continuing to climb through a stance, thereby becoming the leader. If both climbers are of more or less equal competence, this is an efficient way to climb.

ledge: a level area on a cliff or mountain; may be grass, rock, or snow.

load capacity: the maximum load that a piece of gear can withstand.

locking carabiner: see *screwgate*.

manteling: a technique in which the climber moves up high enough to push down on a ledge with both hands until the body is supported on stiffened arms. The climber then replaces one hand with a high-stepping foot and moves up to stand on the ledge.

multipitch route: a climb consisting of more than one pitch.

natural anchor: a tree, boulder, or other natural feature that is well placed and strong enough to make a good anchor.

natural line: a rock climb that follows an obvious feature up the face of a cliff, such as a groove, a gully, or a series of cracks.

niche: a small recess in a rock face, usually large enough to hold a climber.

nose: a jutting protrusion of rock, broad and sometimes with an undercut base.

nut: an artificial chockstone, usually made of aluminum alloy and threaded with nylon cord. Nuts are fitted into cracks in the rock and usually can be used in place of pitons, which can scar the rock. A climber using only nuts needs no hammer, since nuts can be lifted out of their placements.

objective dangers: mountain hazards that are not necessarily the result of flaws in a climber's technique. They include avalanches, rockfall, and crevasses.

off-finger crack: a crack too wide to finger jam, but too narrow to hand jam.

off-hand jam: a crack too wide to hand jam, but too narrow to fist jam.

off-width: a crack that is too wide to fist jam, but too narrow to fit the whole body into.

off-width protection: chocks that are wide enough to anchor in an off-width.

on-sight: to climb a route with no previous knowledge of its moves, except for what one can gain from an observation period.

open book: same as *dihedral.*

opposing chock: a chock that is anchored in the opposite direction from another chock. In combination, the two chocks protect against a multi-directional load.

overhang: rock that exceeds 90 degrees.

palming: a friction hold in which the climber presses the palm of the hand into the rock.

pedestal: a flat-topped, detached pinnacle.

peg: see *piton.*

pendulum: a sideways movement across a rock face by swinging on a rope suspended from above.

pin: see *piton.*

pinnacle: a partially detached feature, like a church steeple.

pitch: a section of climbing between two stances or belay points. A climbing distance that is usually the length of a 150- or 165-foot rope, it is the farthest the leader will go before allowing the second on the rope to catch up.

piton: a metal wedge hammered into a crack until it is secure, used as an anchor point for protection or aid. In the United States, pitons are used only when absolutely necessary, because repeated use damages rock. The first hard-steel pitons were made by John Salathé for use on the Southwest Face of Half Dome in 1946. Also known as *pin* or *peg.*

pocket: a shallow hole—and thus hold—in the rock.

power: strength-to-weight ratio, and thus not simply dependent on muscle size.

problem: a climbing challenge. It is most applicable to shorter climbs, as in a "bouldering problem."

protection: the anchors—such as chocks, bolts, or pitons—to which a climber connects the rope while ascending.

protection system: the configuration of anchors, runners, carabiners, ropes, harnesses, and belayer that combine to stop a falling climber.

prow: a rock feature resembling the prow of a ship, such as the Nose of El Capitan.

put up: to make the first ascent of a route.

rack: the collection of climbing gear carried by the lead climber, as arranged on a gear sling. Also, to arrange the gear on the sling.

rappel: to descend by sliding down a rope. Friction for controlling the descent is provided by wraps of rope around the body or by a mechanical rappel device. The rope is usually doubled so that it can be pulled down afterward. Also called *abseil*.

rappel device: see *descender*.

rappel point: the anchor for a rappel— that is, what the rope, or the sling holding it, is fastened to at the top.

rating system: a system of terms or numbers describing the difficulty of climbs. There are seven major rating systems, including the American (Yosemite) Decimal, British, French, East German, and Australian systems.

redpoint: to lead a climb without falling or resting on aid, usually after a climber has already worked or rehearsed the moves on the route.

rib: a prominent, slender feature, more rounded than an arête.

rock-climbing boots: soft boots with flat rubber soles designed to grip rock.

roof: an overhanging section of rock that is close to horizontal. Roofs vary in size from an eave of a few centimeters to giant cantilevers several yards wide.

rope: important element of the belay system. Modern climbing rope is 150 or 165 feet of nylon kernmantle. Lead ropes range from 9.8 to 11 millimeters in diameter, double ropes 8 to 9 millimeters. According to John Forrest Gregory in *Rock Sport*, the ideal climbing rope would have all the following qualities: low impact force, low elongation under both impact force and low load, good handling qualities, light weight, water resistance, high ratings for holding falls, resistance to cutting and abrasion, and a low price.

roped solo climbing: free-climbing or aid-climbing a route alone but protected by a rope. This is an advanced, complicated technique.

route: a particular way up a cliff. A cliff may have dozens of routes, each with a name and a rating.

runner: a short length of nylon webbing or accessory cord tied or stitched to form a loop; used for connecting anchors to the rope and for other climbing applications. Also called a *sling*.

runout: a section of a climb that is unprotectable, other than with bolts (which may be discouraged).

safety margin: the amount of extra strength built into climbing gear. For example, a carabiner may have a strength rating of 6,000 pounds, but it rarely has to support more than 3,000 pounds. Thus it has a cushion, or safety margin, of 3,000 pounds.

sandbagging: misrepresenting the difficulty of a climb, rating it easier than it really is.

scoop: an indentation in the rock face, not as deep as a niche.

scramble: an easy climb, usually without a rope. (Contrasted with *technical climbing*.)

scree: a long slope of loose stones on a mountainside.

screwgate: a carabiner that can be "locked" with a barrel on a screw thread. Less common than snap-links, screwgates are used when there is a risk of the gate opening. Also called a *locking carabiner*.

seam: a crack far too thin for fingers but big enough to accept some small chocks or pitons.

second: the climber who follows the lead. Though the lead might take a substantial fall, the second usually risks only a short fall, as the belay is from above. The second usually cleans the pitch.

self-belay: the technique of protecting oneself during a roped solo climb, often with a self-belay device.

sewing-machine leg: violent shaking in the leg resulting from holding a bent-knee position too long.

slab: large, smooth rock face inclined between 30 and 60 degrees.

sling: see *runner.*

smearing: a technique of friction climbing used on steep, scooped holds, where the sole of the boot is squashed into the depression to gain the best hold.

snap-link: a carabiner with a spring-loaded gate that opens inward. (Contrasted with *screwgate*.)

soloing: climbing alone, whether roped or unroped, aided or free.

spike: a finger of rock.

stance: the position a climber is in at any given time, especially the position of the belayer.

stemming or bridging: a climbing technique in which the climber pushes out to the sides with hands and/or feet, using opposing pressure against the rock. Often used in ascending chimneys and dihedrals.

stopper: a wedge-shaped nut.

taking in: removing slack in the active rope from a moving climber.

talus: the weathered rock fragments that accumulate at the base of a slope.

technical climbing: climbing that requires hardware, harnesses, ropes, and specialized climbing boots. (Contrasted with a *scramble*.)

third-classing: free-soloing a Class 4 or Class 5 route without protection.

toe hooking: a climbing technique in which a toe is hooked around a rock edge or plastic hold.

top rope: a rope anchored above a climber, providing maximum security; sometimes called *TR*. To top-rope means to rig a climb with a top rope or to climb a pitch using a top rope.

traverse: horizontal movement across a rock face or artificial wall; to proceed around rather than straight over an obstacle; to climb from side to side. A traverse may be an easy walk along a ledge or a daunting passage. Protecting traverses is often difficult, because a fall will cause the climber to pendulum, ending up off-route even if no injuries occur.

tunnel vision: seeing only a small area directly in front. This is a common pitfall for the beginning climber, who, because of nervousness, may miss an obvious hold that is nearby but off to one side.

unidirectional anchor: an anchor that will hold securely if loaded from

one direction but will pull free if
loaded from any other direction.

waist belay: a method of taking in and
paying out a belayed active rope.
The belayer passes the rope around
his waist; the hand on the active
rope side is the directing hand, and
the hand on the slack rope side is
the braking hand. Also called the *hip
belay* or *body belay*.

wall: a steep cliff or face, between 60 and
90 degrees.

Resources

The American Sport Climbers Federation (ASCF) is the governing body for competitive climbing in the United States.

The ASCF does the following:

- Maintains the national ranking of competitive climbers.
- Maintains the national ranking of junior competitors.
- Provides training for competition judges.
- Provides rules and information necessary to run an event.
- Sanctions events that meet requirements.
- Helps promoters raise money for events through promotional activities, such as trying to expand television coverage.
- Registers U.S. competitors for World Cup events.
- Names the U.S. Climbing Team.
- Provides a newsletter four times a year to update members on new rules, rankings, upcoming events, and other ASCF-related activities.

The ASCF also offers its dues-paying ($25 annually) members a discount at ASCF-sanctioned competitions. ASCF members ranked in the top thirty in the nation are entitled to a free one-day pass at participating gyms throughout the United States.

For more information, contact executive director Hans Florine, ASCF, 35 Greenfield Dr., Moraga, CA 94556, telelephone or fax (510) 376-1640.

For Junior information, contact Matt Stevens, 6775 S.W. 111th Ave., Beaverton, OR 97005, telephone (503) 644-3517, fax (503) 222-9109,

E-mail MstevASCF@AOL.COM.

For World Cup information, contact Diane Russell, 1110 Whitewater Cove, Santa Cruz, CA 95062-2888, telephone (408) 479-1801, fax (408) 454-9269.

For information on judging, contact Jim Link, 12404 Kingsley, Louisville, KY 40229, telephone (502) 957-4486.

The ASCF is also on the Internet. Its home page is http://WWW.climbnet.com/ASCF.

ASCF results and other related information can also be found in *Rock and Ice* and *Climbing* magazines.

If you're interested in attending a clinic with Robyn Erbesfield, contact her at Le Cayrounet, 82140 St. Antonin, FRANCE, telephone 011-33-5-63-68-27-10, fax 011-33-5-63-68-27-88. In the United States, contact 5960 River Chase Circle, Atlanta, GA 30328, telephone (770) 955-1711, fax (770) 955-8711.

Sponsorship

A sponsor's relationship with a well-known athlete is quite simple: The sponsor pays the athlete to train, and in exchange, the sponsor has the right to use the athlete's image in advertisements, posters, and other publicity. The athlete may also be asked to appear at trade shows or other sales events.

If you're ready to become a professional climber, you can contact various corporations to apply for sponsorship. The following corporations sponsor Robyn Erbesfield. *Catar* is not pictured below.

Proud to provide the energy for Robyn to reach and remain at the top!

Call for our free color catalog: 303-443-8710, or see our complete line on the web at http://www.sportiva.com